From Oy to Joy
. . . .
Our Holidays Across the Years

*The printing of this book was made possible
by generous contributions from*

Shirley Gould—
in honor of her eighty-fifth birthday;

Elaine Hirsch—
*"to the Jewish Reconstructionist Congregation
and the Reconstructionist Movement
for helping me sustain my Jewish spirit."*

From Oy to Joy

Our Holidays Across the Years

JRC Press • Evanston, IL

*Editors: Mel Patrell Furman, Carol Kanter, and
        Adrienne Lieberman*

Design and Production: Darlene Grossman

Published by JRC Press, 303 Dodge Avenue, Evanston, IL 60202-3252
847.328.7678
fax 847.328.2298
www.jrc-evanston.org

ISBN: 0-9676415-3-5

Printed in the United States of America.

For
Dale Good
whose energies brought JRC Press into being,
whose spirit enlivened so many holidays,
and whose voice joined with all of ours in song.

May his memory be a blessing for us all.

Also by the JRC Press:

Is God a Cubs Fan?
 by Arnold B. Kanter
 with illustrations by Darlene Grossman
 and Cubs season summaries by Sam Eifling

Pirkei Imahot: A Celebration of Our Mothers
 edited by Mel Patrell Furman, Carol Kanter,
 Adrienne Lieberman, and Lynn Pollack

Contents

• •

Foreword

● ●

"You have given us, ALMIGHTY ONE, our God,
in love, the festivals for happiness,
the holidays and seasons for rejoicing."
—from the Jewish liturgy

"You cut the turkey without me?!!"
—from the movie *Avalon*

Cultural anthropologists tell us that holidays offer a window into
a community's soul. Through the rituals of our sacred and civil
festivals, we participate in a kind of mythic drama, a living history
by which our collective past is ever new and ever present. So, if
you want to understand a community, examine its holidays. They
are where a people's innermost beliefs, values, hopes, and
dreams ultimately reside.

But while holidays undeniably express the soul of the collective,
they also have an intensely personal dimension. Just take a
moment to recall the most important, most vivid memories in
your own life. I'd be willing to wager that a significant number of
them are holiday memories. Indeed, when we look back across
the paths we have traveled, holidays stand as signposts on life's

journeys. Leaving indelible imprints on our souls, they serve as sacred touchstones for our lives.

This is not a book about holidays, not really. It is, rather, a testament to the power of memory. And like memory itself, it resonates with oddly familiar tastes and smells and sounds, with joy and heartache, with celebration and sadness. A cultural anthropologist might claim that this remarkable collection provides insight into our congregational community and its collective past. But I think you will also find, as I did, that it will help you to recall your own sacred signposts.

May all of our holiday memories be for a blessing.

—Rabbi Brant Rosen

Introduction

••

Here we are again! After the success of our first two books, *Is God a Cubs Fan?* and *Pirkei Imahot: A Celebration of Our Mothers,* we present *From Oy to Joy: Our Holidays Across the Years.*

We chose to focus this collection on holidays for several reasons. Holidays offer crucial milestones. They serve as a way to organize our memories—times we want to remember and those we wish we could forget. Through holidays we connect with each other and establish and pass on our traditions. We all have holiday stories.

The short stories, essays, poems, and photographs in this book were contributed by members of the Jewish Reconstructionist Congregation. These fifty-eight voices represent as many perspectives and moods. They cover much history and geography. They encompass the religious and the secular, and they range from home to work to places of worship; from old traditions to those newly created (or, some might say, reconstructed); from breakfast to dinner; and from soup to nuts. These stories and poems document the myriad ways people have searched for or created meaning, while celebrating, reminiscing about, and transmitting their most cherished memories.

A note on spelling: We have preserved each author's original spelling of transliterated Hebrew and Yiddish words when these spelling variations indicate different English pronunciations, such as *Shabbat* and *Shabbos,* or when they are used as proper nouns, such as *Bubbe* or *Bubbie.* Definitions of transliterations and other italicized words can be found in the Glossary beginning on page 169.

Like a Passover *Seder,* a project such as this takes the work of many hands. Thank you to the following people who participated in the work of publishing this book and putting it into your hands: project coordinator and copy editor Diane Melnick, whose thoughtful, calm manner and gentle nudging kept everyone anxiety-free and on schedule; our editorial triumvirate, Mel Patrell Furman, Carol Kanter, and Adrienne Lieberman, whose diligence, devotion, and talent shine through the lines on these pages; Darlene Grossman, who designed and produced the book and in countless ways helped nurture the project to fruition; Rabbi Brant Rosen, who crafted another illuminating foreword; the JRC Board of Directors, President Bruce Kaskel, and Executive Director Bryna Cytrynbaum, who gave this project their unwavering support; Syd Lieberman, our storyteller and master of ceremonies, who set the pieces in order; Jeff Winter, who defined the words and terms for our glossary; Carol Friedman, whose careful proofreading insured the quality of this manuscript; all those who helped with the celebratory book launch, sales, and promotions; and especially the JRC contributors who shared their memories and images with such honesty, generosity, and skill.

Along with these stories we offer a challenge to you, the reader. We hope the pieces in this book will inspire you to revisit your own photo album and share your gleanings with family and friends. We all have unique experiences and perceptions and should take advantage of every opportunity to connect with each other through the stories of our lives. So, please make a gift of this book, tuck in your own contribution in the form of a written piece or photo, and ask the recipient to share his or her own holiday story with this traditional toast: *L'chaim,* "to life"!

*Sadie and Simon Esko, grandparents
of Larry Goldberg, c. 1958*

The Fish Is Good This Year

by Larry Goldberg

It was tricky taking out the garbage in those days. Not early in the morning when the galvanized steel garbage can sat empty alongside the Western United Farm box filled with several glass bottles of whole milk. After school, though, was a different matter. On one of those days, staring back from a bed of onion skins and eggshells, lay the glassy eyes of a half dozen fish, some complete with filleted skeletons. With my mom Inez's help, Grandma Sadie was making the *gefilte fish*.

In the kitchen, the women prowled with their aprons securely tied. Their special kitchen equipment came out only for this occasion. The heavy, old cast-iron grinder was clamped to the edge of the counter, its black wooden handle sticking out and the wooden pusher stick at hand. The huge wooden bowl was for finely chopping onions with that peculiar knife blade with the black rounded handle. Along the back counter stood boxes of Manischewitz® *Matzo* Meal with the orange label, the sole manufactured ingredient. And then the big mixing bowls and those wondrous cooking pots, giant enamel affairs with a swirling gray-blue pattern, the heavy lids with their small black knobs perched imperially in the center.

At this ritual, center stage was claimed by the fish. First Grandpa Simon hand-selected each one. Every year a debate ensued about the right proportions of whitefish, pike, trout. Would the finished fish be light or heavy? Would it fall apart from too much moisture or hold together just so? Those fish came whole, only the guts and the scales imperfectly removed at the Chicago Sanitary Fish Store on Argyle, where Grandpa and his brothers toiled. The final scaling, the filleting, and that wondrous grinding would all be done in the kitchen at home.

The work began early in the morning after the kids had left for school. By the time I returned, the house was filled with that fishy holiday smell. The pots boiled with the fish skeletons, as the grinding of fish and onions neared completion. And then the blending began, adding in turn some fish, some water, some egg, some onion, some *matzo* meal, until Grandma said it felt right. Only then could we form the balls from the quivering mound.

Drop, drop, drop: into the water each hand-formed piece would go, there to cook for hours. Before Grandma and Mom were done, the cooked fish had been put back into cleaned pots and covered with broth. In the morning, the fish balls were immersed in that mysterious gelatinous liquid. Where had it come from?

When Grandma became infirm, the duties transferred to Aunt Ruthie's, where the process was hidden from view. The fish would arrive on the evening of *Erev Pesach* or *Erev Rosh Hashanah,* still in those big cast enamel pots, still in that magic gel. But the all-day ritual of cooking could only be surmised. Ruthie didn't care for visitors when she cooked.

The wheels of time turn, and I knew Ruth would not be cooking indefinitely. After a one-year apprenticeship in her kitchen and the passage of a respectful length of time, the ritual finally arrived at my house. Gone were the heavy grinder, those lovely wooden bowls, and the chopping knives. The cooking pots had disappeared as well, distributed somewhere within the family or discarded by the unromantic. The fish, however, goes on.

These days the man at the fish counter at Jewel or Happy Foods selects the whole fish, which he cleans and scales, fillets and grinds. I order some combination of whitefish, pike, and trout, performing the calculations for how many pounds net or gross. "Save the heads and skeletons," I remind him. "I need those to make the broth." Now it all comes in a tidy white package. Chopping the onions, once an ordeal of several hours, is reduced to twenty minutes, compliments of the food processor. And, we store the fish in a huge Tupperware container instead of those ancient pots.

But some things never change. The house still has that smell, and it is still the chief cook's hands that sense the right texture and exactly when to form the balls and drop them, one by one, into the boiling broth. The sink still fills with bowls and pots. The stove is still a mess. And the magic of the gel continues to elude me. On holiday plates, with a few carrot slices for color, and both red and white horseradish, the *gefilte fish* still makes its proud procession from the kitchen, carefully placed by the inheritor of the recipe.

Just as always, though, each year's tastes a little different. Someone comments that the fish is good this year, a little less salty than last year, and both firm and moist. Someone else asks, "Did it take long to make it? Where did you get the fish this year? Will there be enough left for the second night?" There is no comparison with the store-bought fish, squeezed into those tall bottles with the Manischewitz label. Instead, we have the memories, the warm feeling of Grandma Sadie and her kitchen, the honoring of a long-held tradition. Seconds, anyone? ●

Trudel Grossman's matzo-ball soup, Pesach 1968

Matzo Balls To Die For

by Harry Goldin

When my father's mother, my grandmother Leah, found preparing for the family *Seder* too much for her, the responsibility fell on my mother. My grandmother had set the family standard for the perfect *k'neidel* or *matzo* ball: hard as a rock. To please the family, my mother sought to emulate this standard. She worked hard to unlearn her own mother's technique and avoid the pitfalls of making the light and fluffy *matzo* balls of her childhood.

Passover came. Among the guests at my mother's debut *Seder* were two Jewish soldiers from Fort Knox. It was time for the soup. My mother anxiously went around the table and filled each bowl with her steamy chicken soup and "perfect" *matzo* balls. She had worked hard, and now she waited for her husband's and mother-in-law's nods of approval.

Suddenly there was a thud. Then a second and a third. The soldier sitting next to me had tried to cut his *matzo* ball. It was so hard, it had shot out of his bowl onto the floor and bounced several times. My mother had succeeded beyond all expectations. She had surpassed her mother-in-law and set a new standard of excellence for *k'neidlach.* ●

Whatever Happened to Cousin Eddie's Cookies?

by Ken Ross

••

*W*e had invited more than thirty people to our *Seder,* so we posted our kids at the door to get late arrivers seated before sundown. When Cousin Eddie came up the walk carrying a tray of Jewel Bakery chocolate chip cookies, Alex ran to unseal the box we kept under the basement stairs to store our *chametz,* and Mike fetched leather fireplace mitts. As Eddie came through the door, Mike snatched the tray and, holding it between his mitts like a biohazard, rushed it to the basement. Eddie asked Alex if this year his cookies would make it to the dessert table. She shrugged, whispering to her brother: "Maybe in eight days. You'd think the *matzo* would give him a hint."

My wife, Terese, shuttled between a brisket in the kitchen and a gathering of aunts in the dining room. She wore her traditional Passover apron. It said: "Why is this night different from all other nights? Don't ask." Aunt Malkie dogged her steps. Malkie met her first husband in Birkenau, and my Uncle Sammy fifty years later at a singles dance in Boca Raton. Malkie was enamored of Terese, whom she called "Derreeza," touched that this pretty Italian girl would join her family and then choose to join her people. Malkie understood the ramifications of both choices, which moved her to disclose her secret brisket recipe to Terese on our wedding day. For this, and for the homemade *gefilte fish* she brought each year, Malkie had license to follow Terese between oven and buffet counter, singing a heavily-accented "My Yiddishe Mama" over the cacophony of my mom and Aunt Goldie rehearsing *"Dayenu"* by the wine bottles.

Aunt Betty paced the dining room, testing the seal on her Tupperware container. It used to be ours, and every year Betty duly returned it, only to fill it with Malkie's fish for the ride home. Betty's husband, Uncle Bernie, studied our *Haggadah,* scowling. In the early eighties, when my Reconstructionist *shul* published its own *Haggadah,* our social action committee was addressing the plight of Central American refugees. Bernie was a traditional Jew. While Mom and Goldie nipped at the as-yet-unblessed Manischewitz, Bernie donned his purloined funeral home *yarmulke* and fretted because sundown was approaching without the candles lit. He didn't know what to make of the Reconstructionist Exodus story. "What," Bernie asked as I urged some guests to their seats, "were Nicaraguans doing in ancient Egypt?"

I had no time to answer. Cousin Dick arrived and needed a hand getting Aunt Ruth up our front steps. Ruth's mind and body were failing. For forty years, Ruth had brought our family together every spring, set her long, elegant table according to tradition, and sighed resignedly as her younger brother, my Uncle Sid, rushed through a seven-minute *Seder* of his own design. As a hostess, Ruth was grace itself. She'd glide like a dancer from guest to guest, making sure everybody was comfortable in her home, every need fulfilled, everyone feeling special. But now she needed a walker and her son to remind her who and where she was.

Until Ruth's years forced her to surrender the first night of Passover to Terese and the *Seder* to me, Sid was the family's *Seder* leader. Sid was proud of his efficient approach to Jewish ritual. He had edited his Maxwell House® *Haggadah* down to a few prayers and boasted that we'd be eating our second helping of Malkie's fish before the rest of the North Shore Jews got to their seventh plague. But Sid never omitted the 114th Psalm. He loved the phrase, "the mountains skipped like rams, the hills like young lambs." It reminded him of Israel. The spring after Sid made *aliyah*, he expanded his rendition of Exodus to twelve minutes, with the Israelites stopping at every site that Sid visited along the way. As I hurried to meet Aunt Ruth, Sid complained that our *Seder* would last too long and that the Reconstructionists probably cut out the 114th Psalm in favor of some Nicaraguan folk song.

Sundown was near. Almost no one was seated. The dining room was in disarray, and chairs and tables blocked the progress of Ruth's walker. Ruth struggled to her chair next to mine, looking tired and confused.

I watched my family circle the table as I tried to start the *Seder*. Glasses shook as they seated themselves, chairs bumping the table as they continued their loud, animated dialogues. Mike sat in a corner, eyes shut tight, rehearsing the Four Questions, while Alex gave crayons to her younger cousins to color in the Central American farmers depicted on the backs of their *Haggadot*. Malkie reminded Terese to slice the brisket across the grain. Betty inspected the fish. Eddie fruitlessly searched the dessert table for his lost cookies. Mom and Goldie hummed *"Dayenu"* in a weird, discordant tune. Sid griped that we'd probably recite all Ten Plagues; Bernie grumbled, "In Spanish."

I thought of Exodus and the nation of Israel, hundreds of thousands of Jews milling around the banks of the Red Sea. I pictured our ancestors glancing nervously at Pharaoh's chariots, poised to thunder down from Egyptian hilltops, each Jew wondering which of them would take the first step as the Almighty parted the waters.

Ruth tapped her wine glass with a fork. "Sidney, hush up. Kenny has something to say." The room fell silent; people took their seats and looked to me.

"Welcome to our *Seder*," I began, as Terese rose to light the candles. "*Seder,* of course, means 'order'. . ."

The fog lifted from Ruth's eyes, which now seemed as thoughtful as they had been forty years ago. She turned to me and winked. "Isn't that interesting?" she whispered. "You wouldn't think that order was a particularly important Jewish tradition. You wouldn't think that at all." ●

Taking a Pass on Passover

by Adrienne Lieberman

*I*t had been a terrible, horrible, no-good year. Very bad, too. In January 1996, Syd and I consoled ourselves with the prospect of a spring trip to New Orleans. I longed for gourmet meals featuring seafood and my favorite comfort-food dessert: bread pudding swimming in hard sauce.

But my heart sank when I learned that our vacation–timed to coincide with Syd's spring break from teaching–would overlap with Passover. Could we indulge our worldly appetites then, even if we desperately needed release from our own private Egypt? After all, we had been eating the bread of affliction all year. Suddenly the seafood I loved seemed even more forbidden, and my dream of daily bread pudding almost obscene.

You should understand that I fast every *Yom Kippur*. I put spare change in the *tzedakah* box and send checks to charity every month. I try to get to *minyan* on *Shabbat*. And, I especially look forward to Passover: unpacking my glass plates, crying over the fresh horseradish, preparing enough *farfel* granola to last all week, and even essaying home-made *gefilte fish*. Since early adulthood I had never missed a Passover *Seder*. Not only that, Passover meant *matzo*, which I have never liked and therefore have always considered my brown badge of courage. Even in grammar school in Silver Spring, Maryland, where I was the only Jew in class, I brought *matzo* sandwiches, courting humiliation when the rounds of salami fell out and rolled down the class-room aisle.

But I had also grown up with a taste for forbidden food, especially seafood. My mother kept kosher for my father. He had grown up in an Orthodox home, and he never ate meat in a restaurant. Still, he showed amazing tact and restraint when our family dined out. We could always have whatever we wanted. We never pushed our luck and ordered pork, but I ate fried shrimp every chance I got.

My parents' laissez-faire strategy paid off. I still don't eat *treif* at home. My older sister and next younger brother went me one better and don't eat *treif* out either.

I had tried to eat *treif* on Passover once when I was about eight. On a Brownie Scout cookout, the leaders had brought bacon and white bread, and I determined to taste both forbidden foods. My rationalization went like this: I'm away from home, where I can eat whatever I want; I've never tried bacon before and it smells wonderful; if I eat bacon, forbidden every day of the year, I may as well have bread, too, since it's forbidden only this week.

But in my careful calculation of sin, I hadn't counted on Marjorie Levin's mother. Mrs. Levin knew I was Jewish, and she had brought *matzo* for Marjorie and me. Would you have asked for bacon on *matzo* under the watchful gaze of your mother's friend? I didn't either.

My father died many years ago, but I feel his presence most keenly on Passover. In a droning voice he *davened* every word of the Maxwell House® *Haggadah*. Meanwhile, we kids vied to find the outrageous misspellings, gulped enough Manischewitz to pretend we were drunk, raced to capture the *afikomen,* and sang as loud as we dared.

These days at our own *Sedarim,* everyone participates in the prayers and readings. And our beautiful *Haggadot* have no typos. Each year we celebrate the first *Seder* at a different house. At my brother's we learn new Yiddish songs, and the service goes very late. At my sister's we discover feminist readings and discuss world events. When it's my turn, there's usually a role-play or a group art project. No matter where we are, though, my father's spirit hovers nearby. My mother, sister, and brothers feel it, too.

But that year, that very bad year, my father's spirit was telling me that when I was out, I could do as I pleased. And I knew that I needed to be out. Out of *Mitzrayim* and out of feeling blue. I hated missing our family's *Seder,* but that Passover in New Orleans, my personal feast of freedom tasted divine.

I could even feel my father's spirit hovering nearby. In the family lore, my father had taken a trip to New Orleans before my parents were married. It was hard to imagine my ascetic father choosing such an epicurean destination, but we were told he went to Antoine's, a fabled New Orleans restaurant, where he ordered his usual fish. The waiter delivered it with a flourish. Then my father did the unthinkable: he asked for ketchup. Speechless, his waiter swept out of the room. A few minutes later the chef emerged from the kitchen, stormed my father's table, and slammed down an enormous tray rattling with condiments. "There," he sneered in a French accent. "Fix it yourself."

I trust that my father, who had once committed this outrageous act in New Orleans, gazed down with compassion on his wayward daughter, committing another. ●

Remembering Grandpa

by Howard Friedland

When I was growing up, *Pesach* was always a special time in our house, because my grandfather and uncle would make one of their twice yearly visits. They lived in the Upper Peninsula of Michigan, in a town called Iron River, where the snow stops falling sometime in mid-July and starts falling again the first of August. So my grandfather and uncle were always glad to welcome spring in downstate Illinois.

My most vivid memory of *Pesach* is Grandpa making *matzo brei*. Although the *matzo brei* itself tasted great, it is the preliminaries that stand out. Like clockwork, Grandpa would rise early every morning of *Pesach* to begin his search for the perfect skillet to use for frying *matzo*. Now, Mom had about four skillets, of varying sizes, which hung on the inside door of one of our kitchen cabinets. Grandpa would open the cabinet at 6 A.M. each day to retrieve his skillet of choice, and the clanging of pots and pans could be heard throughout the house—like the sound of church bells heard in small towns on Sunday mornings. Awakened by the clamor, we would scamper into the kitchen where Grandpa stood with a piping-hot pan of *matzo brei*.

Grandpa was five feet tall by five feet wide, built like a teamster with no fat. His shirt sleeves were held up with elastic

Howard Friedland with his grandfather, Sam Stein, 1963

bands (he had to buy a large neck size, so the arms were always too long). He ate an apple with a knife, methodically peeling away all of the skin first. He had been born in Lithuania at the end of the nineteenth century and could converse in five languages though he had only a few years of formal education. He was a dealer in livestock who never made much money, and what he did have, he spent on everyone but himself. A pious Jew, Grandpa was accepting of other Jews and other customs. He always said "hello" to people, whether he knew them or not. He took care of my mentally disabled uncle by himself, and he did it with love and patience.

Grandpa had come to this country as Tzelic Mayefsky at age thirteen, without his parents, to live with an older sister in a Polish Catholic mining town in the Upper Peninsula. The man who now stood in our kitchen was known as Sam Stein. It was a simple name for a simple man, whose life was uncluttered with material things and whose greatest commodity was love. ●

*Margaret Lurie with her mother, Augusta Rickover Berman,
and brother, Larry, Starved Rock, Illinois, Columbus Day 1952*

The Great Unwashed

by Margaret Lurie

*T*hey say that cleanliness is next to godliness. My family would have to agree.

My brother Larry, who was unusually precocious, enrolled in the University of Chicago at age fifteen, during the radical 1960s. He quickly got caught up in anti-war protest activities. He also looked the part—raggedy clothes, long unkempt hair, unshaven, and, it seemed to our family, unwashed.

On Passover, he would come up to our house on the North Side of Chicago for the *Seder*. There was great anticipation every year within the large family group gathered around the table. At one point in the service, my grandfather would instruct all of us to follow the ritual of washing our hands.

With much excitement and many jokes, the entire family would follow my brother into the kitchen and watch as he scrubbed his hands.

Even though Larry is fifty-four years old today and is absolutely immaculate, when the first of the Four Questions is asked, "Why is this night different from all other nights?", the traditional family answer persists: "Because this is the only night Larry has clean hands." ●

The Root of Passover

by Jeff Winter

*P*assover is a rich blend of sense memories, the sounds and smells of housecleaning and careful preparation of traditional dishes. In our home the most memorable sensory experience blossoms with preparing the bitter herb known in Hebrew as *maror.*

Maror reminds us of the slavery our ancestors suffered three thousand years ago in Egypt. Before celebrating the joy of liberation, we eat bitter herbs in order to relive the difficulty of servitude. Today, for the bitter herb, most people buy commercially prepared horseradish, which one lightly dollops onto *matzo*—or, for the faint of palate, discreetly consumes with sweet apple *charoset.* In the Winter home, however, *maror* is another matter entirely.

Our *maror* is prepared from scratch. The process begins a day before the *Seder,* when I bring home a sapling-sized stem of raw horseradish. I *schlep* the food processor up from the basement while my kids set out jars of vinegar and beet *borscht,* and I begin to peel and chop the root.

Windows stand wide open, regardless of outside temperature, and we don swimming goggles in cautious respect for the impending fumes. I puree chunks of horseradish in the food processor, along with splashes of vinegar and *borscht.* Since only a small portion can be mixed at once, it is critical to make a swift transfer of the *maror* to a bowl and to cover it immediately with a tight lid. Inhaling even a small whiff of the mixture can cause choking and blinding tears. Our team scoops the warm, pink oatmeal-like substance with the crack efficiency of a pit crew at the Indy 500. All squad members hold their breath during the delicate operation lest they have to flee from the room for oxygen. We avoid breathing the "horseradish of death" as though it were the Angel of Death the Israelites feared before their Exodus from Egypt.

Once it cools and settles, we offer portions to friends and family for use at their *Sedarim.* Of course, how they use it is their business. But for us Winters, there is no masking this *maror* under *charoset,* or using it to add a slightly impertinent zest to *gefilte fish.* This is the real deal, sharper than any known spray for clearing the nasal cavity. A powerful reminder of the sting of slavery. We used to quip that *maror* got its name not from *mar,* or "bitterness," but because "the more you eat, the *more* you *roar."*

Why is this night different from all other nights? Because on this night, our sinuses remind us of our roots. ●

Grandma's Way

by Sue Ginsburg

I grew up in a home that was Orthodox, probably out of respect for my grandmother. She was from Brest-Litovsk, a small city on the border of Russia and Poland. After Grandpa died, Grandma came to live with us. She was devoutly religious and an incredible cook. I remember the *challot* she would make every *Shabbos,* as well as her strudel and her *mondel broit.*

And the *gefilte fish* at Passover! It always seemed to reach 85 degrees on the day my grandmother made the *gefilte fish.* She did everything from scratch. She picked out fish at the market, looking at their eyes to make sure they were fresh. She boned them, chopped them, and mixed the different kinds. I wanted to die from the embarrassment when the aroma of fish filled our apartment building. I hated that smell.

I remember her going all around the house with the wing of some bird, collecting *chametz,* making sure the house was ready for the *Seder.* My mom would put all five leaves in the dining room table. There were never fewer than fifteen people for Passover. My dad sat at one head and Grandma sat at the other, presumably to be close enough to the kitchen to watch the chicken soup. My dad always led the *Seder.* My brother, sister, and I always begged him to shorten it, but he never did. He

Sue Ginsburg (front, second from left) and her family with her grandmother, Rose Tormé (directly behind Sue), Chicago, c. 1954

loved leading the service and getting up to wash his hands all those times. Thinking back on it now, I believe it was on one of those hand-washing trips that he chose to hide the *afikomen*.

As my dad led the service, all in Hebrew, another softer voice would issue from the other end of the table. There my grand-mother would sit, conducting her very own *Seder,* paying no attention to what my dad was doing or where he was in the service. She was always a bit behind him, but he would defer to her and wait until she finished before we could eat. He might have rolled his eyes or shaken his head once or twice, but he always respected her need to do it her way. As far as I know, she was the only person who ever challenged my dad and won. ●

The Feldman Family with Ida, Diane Melnick's mother (far right in white), and her brother, Irving (seated in white chair), Zhitomir, Russia, c. 1913

A Shabbos Tale

by Diane Melnick

*W*hen the last czar of Russia sat on his throne, my mother, Ida, was a little girl in the town of Zhitomir. She was petite, with delicate features, and her family thought she didn't look Jewish. So they often sent her to learn the news from Gentile neighbors, especially when Cossacks were rumored to be near. Such rumors frightened the family into hiding, sometimes for days at a time.

On Fridays, Ida often ran one special errand. She put fresh home-baked loaves of *challah* into her wooden wagon. Then she and her older brother, Irving, would walk to their small synagogue to deliver the bread to the rabbi, making sure to return home before *Shabbos* began at sundown.

One Friday, when Ida and Irving entered the synagogue, they were met by an unnatural silence. Tentatively they opened the sanctuary door. There lay the rabbi and his assistant, awash in blood. Ida and Irving fled, leaving behind the *challot,* the wagon, the blood, and the dead. But my mother could never leave behind her memories of this horror. For her they would define *Shabbos* forever.

Decades later, when I was a little girl, our home had no *Shabbos* traditions. My father frowned on overt observance of Jewish ritual, calling himself a "free thinker," and my mother acquiesced to his refusal to bring *Shabbos* into our lives. He insisted that in our hearts we knew we were Jews and therefore did not need the trappings of ritual. My older sister, Adrian, said that we were expected to absorb Judaism through osmosis. But I begged my mother for stories about her childhood. Her *Shabbos* tale became mine. It linked me to her past and to an understanding of what it might mean to risk being Jewish.

As a teenager I defined myself by my studies, and, as a young adult, by my work as an advertising director. My husband, also Jewish, was equally busy with graduate school and research. Both of us regarded Friday night as a welcome break from frenetic schedules. But we didn't rest. We entertained ourselves by going to plays, concerts, restaurants, and movies. I continued to feel that because I was Jewish in my heart, *Shabbos* observance was unnecessary.

Yet I never forgot my mother's *Shabbos* story. Fifteen years into my marriage, when my mother was terminally ill with cancer, I became pregnant. Knowing that I would give birth to a son after she had died, a son who would be named after her according to Jewish tradition, helped me reevaluate her *Shabbos* tale. My husband also encouraged me to rethink my connection to Judaism. How we wished to live and what we wanted to teach our son became clear.

We decided that we would like him to learn and understand what being Jewish was all about, especially the beauty, strengths, and insights of our tradition. Yes, I wanted our son to hear my mother's *Shabbos* tale of fear, trauma, and escape. But I also wanted to go beyond this telling to help shape a life with the joys and blessings of Judaism.

And we let it begin with *Shabbos.* Since Ian's birth, we have welcomed this time of the week in a Jewish way. We no longer seek entertainment or diversion on Friday night. Instead we bring

Shabbos into our home as in generations past, by joining in song, saying *b'rachot,* explaining what we are thankful for, and discussing the week's *Torah* portion. Sometimes we welcome company or go to friends' homes for dinner. More often, we are three guests at our own table, grateful for each other and this beautiful pause from routine weekday pressures. As I light the *Shabbos* candles and their lovely glow enters our lives, I think of my mother. And, I dedicate this new *Shabbos* story to her. ●

Hallie Rosen, Carol Hirsh Blechman, and Beth Lange, July 4, 2000

Independence Day

by Arnold B. Kanter

*J*uly 4th is a big day on my block, the 1200 block of Judson Avenue in Evanston, Illinois. It has been so ever since 1976, the Bicentennial of the founding of our country.

That Bicentennial July, the Kanter family was in the throes of one of our house remodeling projects, which we undertake at intervals sufficient for us to forget our vow never again to undertake another one. The 1976 project involved installing central air conditioning in our turn-of-the-century house, which meant we'd removed all of our window air conditioners, save the relatively new one in the kitchen. We'd kept that one in case the heat generated by cooking in the kitchen proved too much for our new system. As luck would have it, July 4, 1976, was one of those hotter-than-hell Fourths, and our mid-project house was so stifling that my wife, Carol, hit on the idea of all four of us bringing sleeping bags downstairs and spending the night in the kitchen—our sole air-conditioned room.

In mid-June 1976, a bunch of the neighbors on the block had gotten together and decided that the Bicentennial was the perfect time to institute a patriotic tradition—an annual Fourth of July block party. There were big doings. Our street was blocked off, American flags hung from front porches, the fire department provided a big fire truck for us to climb on and ogle (only old fogies like me were disappointed that the truck was yellow, instead of red, as fire trucks are supposed to be), a local real estate company provided free ice cream sandwiches wrapped in paper that advertised their company (you can't get much more American than that), and each family on the block chipped in a couple of bucks to buy soft drinks and a big keg of beer.

But that wasn't all. Every family provided a salad or dessert for the entire block to share and brought their own hot dogs and hamburgers to cook on grills that were rolled out onto the sidewalk. A volleyball net was strung across the street, and kids rode their tricycles or Big Wheels down the center of the street. Uncooked eggs soared across the street from one team member to another at increasing distances until they splattered, either on the street or in a teammate's hands. After dinner, a talent show featured such memorable acts as my six-year-old daughter, Jodi, playing "Twinkle, Twinkle, Little Star" on her one-eighth size violin, and my daughter Wendy, not yet four, singing and mugging with Ellie, her best buddy from down the block. And all of this took place in addition to the big Fourth of July parade down Central Street—which featured floats and bands and politicians—and the gala fireworks show down by the lake as night fell. In short, to say that a good time was had by all would be a major understatement.

The next year, as July 4th approached, with our air-conditioning project long since completed, the weather was, predictably, cool. As June turned to July, we reminded our daughters that we would again be going to see the big Central Street parade and then cele-brating at our gala block party. By the first of July, Wendy, almost five years old now, was just about bursting with excitement, asking each day whether tomorrow was the big day. Secretly proud at the obvious impression that last year's festivities had made on our younger daughter, and curious as to what Wendy was anticipating most, Carol asked her why she was so excited. Without hesitation, Wendy replied, "Ooh, because this is the holiday that we all get to sleep in the kitchen."

Ah, patriotism. ●

"¡María Está Aquí!"

by Jan Yourist

*L*ast summer, I had begun work at a new charter school located next door to a large Catholic Church, a rectory, and a convent. All summer a huge dumpster squatted in the parking lot, collecting the debris of my school's renovation.

"Mary's in there," one of the workman said, pointing at the dumpster. I peered in. There amidst the garbage, pieces of drywall, empty paint cans, and an old washing machine, lay an old marble sculpture, face down. Standing next to it was a base with two feet peering out from beneath a robe, balanced on a globe with a snake wrapped around it.

Mary in the dumpster? How could the church just have thrown her away? Wasn't she considered a sacred icon? Weren't there special ways to dispose of old religious materials? Didn't Catholics have a *geniza*?

I ran into the building and begged some of the workmen to help me get Mary out of the dumpster and into my car. They just laughed. "She must weigh at least a thousand pounds," they said. Besides she was already under quite a bit of debris. It was clear that the thought of digging her out, let alone lifting her out of the dumpster, daunted everyone but me. I resigned myself to the fact that we weren't going to be able to lift Mary out of the dumpster, but I remained determined to save her.

Armed with a borrowed hammer and chisel, I told my son, who was helping me paint and move furniture, that at least we would be able to get her head. Isaac looked at me as if I were crazy. I showed him how to use the tools, and he began to chip away at the marble about her mid-back.

Moments later, a big carpet truck pulled up into the parking lot. After four brawny workers delivered our new carpet, one strode over to the dumpster.

"What are you doing?" he asked Isaac.

"It's the Virgin Mary," I answered. "Can you believe it? They're throwing her out. We're trying to save her."

"Da Virgin Mary?! C'mon guys. Let's help. Open your trunk."

The other three guys walked over to my open trunk, their reluctance growing as they calculated the heavy task before them. But slowly and with much prompting from me, they committed themselves to this holy deed. First, they helped push the washing machine off Mary. Then, with herniated angst, they turned her over and lifted her up.

She was beautiful, even with her nose a bit worn off and most of the fingers missing from her outstretched arms. The guys stepped slowly, grunting, and rested her head on the bumper of my car before one last lift into the trunk.

"Hey, it looks like she's ready for Joseph." I was shocked at this lewd comment.

The carpet man read my glance. "That's all right. I'm Italian. I can say that."

With a final groan, they transferred Mary into my trunk.

"We saved da Virgin," the original volunteer crowed. "That's seven years of good luck." Then they drove off, waving.

I had been watching carefully as Mary's weight sunk my car so low that the wheel well touched the top of the tire. Christ, I thought, there goes the suspension.

María, Winter 2001

That's when I went back into the school to share my dilemma with the other workmen. I was determined that they would help me, and finally they did. One volunteered his van. Then four others came to the car and lifted Mary from my trunk. With much grunting, heaving, and sweating, they placed her into the back of the borrowed van.

Isaac and I had no idea how we would get Mary out of the van and into our backyard. We were definitely going to need more help when we arrived home. But, trusting in our precious cargo and the ways of the universe, we steered our path toward the

North Side. I could hardly waste time worrying about the fact that my car had not risen to its original height after Mary had emerged.

As we pulled into our alley, a plan started to gel in my mind. On that summer afternoon, scattered neighbors hung out on stoops and in backyards. Luckily, our fridge held cold Coronas. I ran outside, waving the bottles to my relaxed neighbors.

"Ven acá. ¡María está aquí! ¡María está aquí!"

Intrigued, they followed me into the alley where Mary lay on her back in the van. Broad smiles crossed their faces, and then they got very serious. Luckily we had mounds of scrap wood in the garage. After I backed the van into the garage, the volunteers constructed a sloping ramp from the back of the van to the back door of the garage. With much coaxing, Mary slid down the ramp into our backyard, gazing up at the sunny sky. We felt happy to have rescued something so beautiful and sacred.

Beers all around. More neighbors looking her over. Then the questions: Will we get her cleaned? Will we put her back together?

Over the next two weeks Mary lay on her back in the yard, too heavy to lift. Pools of water gathered between the sculpted cloth over her head and shoulders and the sides of her neck. On my way to work, I would look at the clouds reflected in these waters.

On several occasions I had to use the fax machine or phone at the church next door. There I ran into the parish priest.

"I heard you saved Mary of the Stumps."

"Stumps?"

"Yeah, that's what I called her. Her fingers were all worn off."

"Well, I couldn't just let her be thrown away. I mean, it's Mary, for God's sake. She's in our garden now."

The priest tried to explain how Mary had come to be in two pieces in the dumpster. "Some crazy guy leaped up on the statue and knocked her over. She cracked into two pieces. We had to hold onto her until the insurance adjusters were finished with all the paperwork. Then I had a couple of kids drag her on boards over to the dumpster. Now we have that fiberglass statue."

His story still didn't make sense to me. But I smiled and thought, "It's pretty amazing that I, a Jewish woman, saved the Virgin Mary and now have her in the middle of our garden. Well, Mary was Jewish, too, wasn't she?"

A few days later, a couple of the nuns from the convent came over to visit my school and admire its transformation.

"We heard you saved the Virgin Mary," one said.

"Yes," I replied. "I couldn't believe they were going to throw her away. Such an indignant and inelegant demise. And in a dumpster yet!"

"Well, the Catholic Church has never treated their women very well."

At the end of the month, my step-daughter Amy, her new husband, and our new in-laws came for a visit. Through a series of ropes, pulleys, and wedges, and our own grunts, heavings, and sweat, our large group finally stood up the footless Virgin.

We continue to argue whether she should be put back together or left in two parts. My husband believes we should put Mary back together. I prefer to leave her in two parts. The base currently sits in our herb garden, holding up a sculpture of Buddha that Isaac made several years ago. In the summer, birds land on Mary's stumps and spiders build webs that connect her to our garage. In the winter, the snow collects on the top of her head like a huge bowler hat.

As a family, we plan to celebrate every July 24th as the day the Virgin Mary came into our garden. We will invite the parish priest and the nuns from the convent. We'll celebrate with a neighborhood barbecue and plenty of Coronas. And, to bewildered Jewish friends, we will simply explain that our family relishes any opportunity to celebrate the rescuing of the sacred. ●

Dump It and Start Over

by Rick Friedman

*W*hen I was growing up, all but one of the aunts I knew were great-aunts, the siblings or in-laws of my mother's parents, Rose and Larry. These were women of strong character and strong opinions, especially Larry's older sister, Aunt Edith. She was married at seventeen and had to endure the loss of her husband and daughter but nevertheless thrived on work, friends, and family. She smoked, she had a mischievous sense of humor, and she made the best *blintzes* and *mondel bread* any of us ever tasted.

About once a month, we had Friday night dinner at my grandparents' apartment. Edith was usually there, too. She would always arrive with a brown paper bundle. We knew what was inside—*mondel bread,* wrapped in reused aluminum foil and covered with a plastic bag. The diagonally cut cookies were both crispy and crumbly, with just enough sugar to keep us interested. We would grab a couple, and then the plastic bag would get twisted and closed. But never for long, for we were the lucky ones. You see, our family consisted of the haves and the have-nots: those with *mondel bread* and those without.

When I graduated from college, Edith was in her late seventies. I knew the *mondel bread* would not come forever.

One afternoon she agreed to teach me her recipe. She lived near the lake in a one-bedroom apartment with barely enough room for both of us to stand in the kitchen at the same time. For her, the routine was second nature. As she spoke, she measured the ingredients: four cups plus two tablespoons of flour, one teaspoon plus a little more of baking soda, a teaspoon of salt. She poured everything into her ancient sifter, with barely a touch of red paint left on the round handle. "Sift it three times," she advised. "Why three?" I asked. A shrug was her only answer.

In a separate bowl, Edith scooped a cup of sugar. "A little more or less doesn't matter." In a life such as hers, exactness did not add much nor inexactness detract at all. Next she added eleven ounces of oil, an odd measurement I had never heard before and haven't heard since. Cracking an egg, she made sure to mix it well with the sugar and oil, then repeated that process three more times. "If the eggs are small, you can add one more." Then Edith slowly added the flour mixture to the larger bowl. Her mixer's motor complained as the dough finished mixing. Taking the beater out of the mixture, she asked whether I wanted to add nuts or chocolate chips.

"No," I answered, "I like it plain."

"Next comes the hard part," she said matter-of-factly. Edith took two black-coated cookie sheets from a drawer and instructed me to smear a little shortening on them. "Make sure your hands are wet and shape the dough into two loaves on each pan. They should only be a couple inches wide, but they can be as long as the pan."

With the pans in the oven, set at 325 degrees, we cleaned up and talked. About thirty-five minutes later Edith took out the pans. The browned loaves were ready to be cut into the famous diagonal shape, about three-fourths inch wide. Then she turned them over on their sides to brown under the broiler. "You have to watch them carefully not to toast them too dark. If it doesn't come out right, just dump it and start over."

She said this with a smile, but I know she meant it. Over the years, I'm sure she probably dumped a batch or two. After they toasted, Edith removed the pans again to turn all the cookies over on the other side to repeat the process. Three minutes later, a perfect batch was ready to cool on wire racks. Edith carefully wrapped the cooled *mondel bread* in a piece of used aluminum foil and put it in a plastic bag. I still have the recipe she wrote out for me in her fluid handwriting.

Some time passed before I made the *mondel bread* alone for the first time. But on the many occasions I have made it since, I always reflect on the woman who shared with me much more than a cookie recipe.

About five years after my visit, Aunt Edith moved to Shreveport, Louisiana, to live in a nursing home near her son and his family. I never saw, wrote, or spoke to her again. In January 2002, the news came that at age ninety-six, Edith had died. She would be buried next to her husband at Waldheim Jewish Cemetery in Chicago.

The small gathering met to bid farewell to Edith. Her grown grandchildren shared personal reflections and stories, which invariably concerned *mondel bread*. While Edith's grandson, David, was telling one such story, he awkwardly pulled a bulky bundle from the pocket of his raincoat. This bag, he said, held *mondel bread* that his grandmother made some fifteen years earlier. The package had been moved from one freezer to another but was still intact. He opened the plastic bag of foil-wrapped cookies and passed it around, insisting that we taste once more, together, the last of Edith's *mondel bread*. With morbid curiosity, we hesitantly sampled the crumbly pieces of *mondel bread*. It was definitely the real thing. After we all took a piece, David dumped the crumbs into the grave, sprinkling the top of the coffin. I tried to decide whether, fifteen years later, hers tasted better than the batch I had hurriedly made that morning for the *shiva* meal.

It didn't. After all, some things hold up over time, while others do not. Traditions, especially family traditions, must be shared in order to survive. So, just as Edith advised so many years ago, I occasionally need to dump a batch of *mondel bread* and start over. Even more important, I try to give the good batches away to family and friends. I expect to make Edith's recipe for a long time. Yet sometimes, while carefully watching the cookies bake, I wonder who will make the *mondel bread* after me. ●

August First—New Year's Day

by Carol Kanter

Who's to say just where a circle ends
   and starts?
Calendars mark January first "New Year's Day"
   world-wide hoopla
      a national holiday
         resolutions a-glitter with hope

But you needn't be a Lincoln, King, or the US of A
   to reckon years
      from birthday to birthday
         hoping to grow one candle wiser

Rosh Hashanah celebrates the Birthday of the World
   usually in September
      but sometimes early, sometimes late
         so *rebbes* must read out when it will fall
         and when the Jewish year runs extra long you're glad
            if all is well
            not so glad if it's a bad spell and you're eager
               to turn over a new leaf already
      hoping for that honey-sweet shalom

A business can decree its fiscal year begins
on any date or imitate
the IRS and pick the Ides of April
hoping to finish well in the black

My husband's Opening Day slides in at Wrigley Field
hoping against hope
(For all we know, his doctor's year starts three days hence
as he fields my husband's hoarse call
to treat his throat
sore from screaming for his Cubbies
in the cold Chicago pitches as Spring)

But my New Year rolls in on August first,
Opening Day for my Literary Year
no arbitrary date, but chosen to precede
a likely trip when I can get a jump
on the stalk of books growing weekly by my bed
without hoopla or moral messages
its invitation tick-tock predictable
to come-as-you-are whatever the weather
And no matter what I have (or have not) read
regardless of how close my numbers climbed to 52
through mid-night yesterday
or how short they fell
at 20
Hoping some rare read will blossom
sparkly on my up-and-coming list
I turn over a fresh notebook leaf
call it a year
and begin anew ●

Phillip and Minnie Marx, grandparents of Eileen Heisler, c. 1930

My Sense of Rosh Hashanah

by Maxine Topper

*G*rowing up as one of the only young Jews in Union Pier, a small town in Southwest Michigan, I often felt like two separate people, one semi-Christian in the winter and the other semi-Jewish in the summer. During the school year, I participated with friends in their church activities and celebrated their holidays. During the summers, the "Chicago people," mostly Jewish, came to enjoy the beach and escape from the city heat. With separate sets of summer friends and winter friends, I never felt as if I quite fit in anywhere.

But each September, shortly after my Chicago friends went home and I reacquainted myself with my schoolmates, my anticipation would grow as the wonder of the High Holidays drew close. I felt totally connected to the small community of Jews who came together there and also connected to Jews around the world who gather each year at this time to pray. The little synagogue, shuttered throughout most of the year, was prepared for the holidays. The few permanent Jewish residents, who remained in Union Pier after the summer season, would call the rabbi, replace the prayer books and *tallitot* on the shelves, dust the seats, and open the doors to families from the city who would return to pray with us.

I still remember the overload of senses that defines that holiday, from the shine of my always-new shoes, to the feel of my father's rough hand holding mine as we proudly walked the few blocks to the synagogue on *Rosh Hashanah.* I had the awesome responsibility of carrying his velvet *tallit* bag, feeling its softness as we walked past the wonderful fall smell of grapes ripening on bushes. To this day, the smell of concord grapes sparks this memory.

Arriving at the synagogue, my father would kiss me and go in. The sight was awesome, but there were so many things I did not understand. Men and women sat in separate sections. The entire service was in Hebrew, except for an occasional directive as to page number. I would slide along the hard wooden benches to find a safe seat near someone I knew and wait for my mom, who was home preparing for the feast. My ears would fill with the hum and mumble that I identified as prayer. The words and symbols in the prayer book were foreign to me. I tried mumbling; I swayed when the congregation did; I wondered what they were saying, what they were feeling. I wanted to feel that, too.

I would focus and wonder, then get bored and run out, looking for someone my age to hang out with. Children were free to rejoin the service at any time.

(This was true on *Yom Kippur* as well, except during that fearful part of the service called *Yizkor* when we were ushered out, the door was closed, and who knew what was going on in there. I later realized that this was the memorial prayer for the dead, in which only "official" mourners participated. As an adult, when I took part in a community *Yizkor* service, I trembled as if I should not be there, lest someone close to me die.)

Although as a child I had no concept of what people were saying, why they were saying it, or what would happen if they didn't, I always watched, fascinated and warmed, in awe as my father performed the rituals along with the others. I especially was entranced when he pulled the huge *tallit* over his head and knelt before the Ark. I loved the times when the *Torah* was carried around the room, and I would rush to kiss it, showing my respect. My father would always stop in front of my row, smiling at me as I reached for the sacred scroll, careful not to touch it directly.

As the day unfolded, my father would sneak a peek over his shoulder every time the door opened. He was waiting for my older siblings and their families to arrive. I still hold an image of my father, beaming as his children and grandchildren entered the synagogue. It's the same feeling I get now when my kids show up and climb into the seat next to me.

Rosh Hashanah dinner was the big family event. My father would hold the glass of wine high to recite the *Kiddush,* bless us all and wish us the sweetness of the new year, pleased as he surveyed the room and saw his family grow year after year. The honey, apples, and *challah* were passed around for all to share. The dinner would begin, the table groaning with traditional foods including, always, my mother's specialty, sweet potato casserole made even sweeter with brown sugar and canned, crushed pineapple, and topped with tons of miniature marshmallows. Most of the dishes and glassware had been collected from bank premiums, gas station giveaways, and old *Yahrzeit* glasses. Nothing matched, but the familiarity of the scene contributed to our sense of belonging. Dinner over, holiday done, we would return to the rhythm of small-town life. ●

Family of Beth Jacoby with her grandmother, "Sally" Schwartz (seated below wall plate on right), the Bronx, New York, c. 1950s

Our "Signature" Dish
by Beth Jacoby

A family's heirlooms not only provide connections to the past but may also offer insights into the family's current behavior. For my family, the heirloom that best symbolizes our cooking style is my grandmother's "Sally" pin. The pin was remarkable, not because it was fine costume jewelry but because my grandmother's name was not Sally. It was Dorothy. Well, actually, it was Golda, but that's another story. However, the pin had been on sale at Abraham & Strauss, and since she could find no Dorothy (or Golda) pins, "Sally" made a perfectly good substitute.

This combination of practicality and creativity carried over into the kitchen, particularly on those special days before *Rosh Hashanah,* when my grandmother would make one of her "signature" apple pies. The whole operation began with the search for useable apples, a formidable task because the vast majority of apples that our backyard tree produced were the shriveled, worm-eaten variety. The few edible exceptions tended to concentrate on the tree's upper branches. Retrieving them was a perilous procedure involving brooms and other household appliances. Eventually, my grandmother would emerge victorious from her battle with our tree, bearing a few pie-worthy specimens.

With the apples safely procured, Grandma could then begin making her pie crust. This recipe was not written down, but instead became part of our family's oral tradition, a sort of culinary *Torah she-be'al peh*. The recipe went something like this: "Take a handful of flour, some butter and vegetable shortening, a little salt, a little sugar. Mix with your hands and add a little water until it feels 'right.'"

While the end result was always tasty, the means to that end was not exactly exact. So, in a desperate attempt to codify Grandma's recipe for posterity, my sister and I devised a plan. We removed anything my grandmother was about to toss, pinch, or sprinkle into the bowl, poured it into measuring cups or spoons, annotated it, and only then put it back into the bowl.

The resulting formula, now committed to paper for all time, reads:

1 cup plus ¼ cup plus another ¼ cup flour

4 Tbsp. plus 1½ Tbsp. butter

2½ Tbsp. plus ½ Tbsp. vegetable shortening

A pinch plus another pinch of salt

A pinch of sugar

About ⅛ cup of water

Proceed as before.

Now, any of us can make my grandmother's pie crust recipe. But, I'm quite certain that the resulting apple pie would never taste the same as hers. Invariably, Grandma would sneak in something else to make it taste different and special. An additional dollop of some ingredient. An extra pinch of a secret spice. Or maybe it was just the fact that *she* made it, proving simply that you can't quantify everything.

Our family considers cooking more an exercise in improvisation than an exact science, and a recipe less an empirical document than a prompt for our creativity. After all, ingredients can be added, deleted, or modified, depending on mood or what's in your cupboard. As my grandmother would say, "How bad could it be?" This philosophy has been encoded in our DNA and transmitted from one generation of my family to the next. My mother, for example, looks at a recipe not for how she can make it but for how she can change it. Which explains why her recipe for Bacardi Rum Pecan Cake is very likely to contain Kahlua, walnuts, and chocolate instead.

This renegade culinary behavior can have disastrous social ramifications. Perplexed and frustrated friends frequently inquire why the dish they made from my mother's recipe tastes nothing like the dish she made for them. Of course, it's because the dish my mother made for them *was* nothing like the recipe.

In an effort to protect herself and her friends from such disappointments, my mother now resorts to evasive maneuvers:

"Doris, how did you make that?"

"Oh, I just threw a few things together."

"I must have the recipe."

"Well, I really didn't use one."

"Come on!"

"Really, I didn't!"

"Oh. So, you're one of those people who doesn't like to *share* recipes."

Of course, this last accusation is tantamount to harboring a terrorist. But I, too, share this family predisposition. Like Mom and Grandma, I can hardly read a dessert recipe without thinking, "Hmm. I bet cinnamon would taste good in this." I guess the apple really doesn't fall far from the tree. Or the pie.

What does this improvising say about us? That we can't follow rules? That we are chronic nonconformists? That we can't play well with others? Perhaps it's simply that the idea of a recipe is just too confining. After all, a recipe is someone else's concept of how something should look and taste. Who says it can't be improved? Our additions embellish a dish with our own imprimatur, inserting a bit of us into the finished product. It's our "signature," written in cinnamon, vanilla, or garlic. It says who we are. Just like a "Sally" pin. ●

*Ruth Horn and Anna Elbaum, Maxine Lange's mother
and mother-in-law, Chicago, November 1958*

Women's Work

by Maxine Lange

When I think about the family holidays of my youth, I think of food—not just eating the ample and delicious meals, but preparing, serving, and cleaning up. This was what the women did. I grew up at a time without dishwashers, microwaves, disposals, or Cuisinarts. Women were in charge of the food. Men didn't cook, and most were not comfortable in the kitchen.

My mother shopped at a variety of stores—the bakery, chicken store, fish store, meat market, fruit market, and small family grocery. There was no supermarket and shopping took forever. In addition, food was packaged differently. For example, poultry was all fresh. I remember having to help pluck the feathers from our fresh turkey. As an adult, it took years before I would eat turkey.

My own big job was setting the table—without a fancy centerpiece or fine china. I also helped my mother bring out the food and serve it. It seemed to take much less time to eat dinner than to prepare it. After dinner, the men discussed politics, sports, and business. Sometimes they played cards.

The women did the cleanup, discussing children, cooking, clothes, family, and sometimes politics as they worked. The kitchen was packed, as all the women helped with the dishwashing and drying. It was like an assembly line, with lots of movement, talking, and laughing. My job was keeping a steady supply of clean dishtowels ready for those assigned to dry the dishes. Although I loved this time in the kitchen and felt almost like an adult, I also felt we were missing something important.

I remember cleaning up after *Rosh Hashanah* dinner in 1948, when the men had a particularly heated discussion about the upcoming presidential election. I was old enough to know what was going on, and I wanted to hear what they were all yelling about. But I was stuck in the kitchen. I couldn't ignore the excitement; nor could I really listen or participate.

The memories of those days are filled with good feelings. However, I'm glad things have changed. While food is still a major item in our holiday celebrations, everyone participates in its preparation, serving, and cleanup. We all discuss politics, sports, work, children, and gossip around the dining room table. ●

The Turning of the Years

by Shirley Gould

"*T*his soup doesn't taste like Ma's." My brother Sid said it at our *Rosh Hashanah* table in 1952, and the hurt simmered for years.

It was hot and I had two toddlers underfoot. Because I lived closest to the synagogue to which my whole family belonged, they all gathered around my table after services. Besides, Joe and I had a big house with plenty of room for everybody.

I was eager to be a *balabusta,* literally a "boss," like Mom, now that she could no longer be the cook and hostess. And I wanted to be a *beryeh,* too–a good housekeeper, capable and skillful in all the womanly occupations. The best part of cooking was having family around my table. As if she hadn't heard Sid, my mother quietly sipped her soup. So did my sisters and their families. I was so hurt that all my hard work was unappreciated, and I thought about Sid's comment many times afterwards.

As children we had been rivals. Sid was born in April 1912, the fourth child and second son, and, I imagine, a welcome prince. A picture of him as a toddler in a white dress shows profuse brunette curls and an adorable smile. When I was born in August 1917, the fifth and last child, Sid was dethroned. I was the kind of baby about whom people said, "This one is going to talk any minute."

With our age gap and the difference in our interests, Sid and I had little to do with one another. I didn't play ball, and he wasn't interested in paper dolls. He didn't want to be seen escorting me to kindergarten, either. As adults, distance separated us. We moved to Skokie, while Sid and his family moved to South Shore. We seldom saw each other.

Many years later, I enrolled in college for the first time. When I got my B.A., the only graduate school that would accept a fifty year old was the Jane Addams School of Social Work. That's where I learned about the famous Contagious Disease Hospital on South California Avenue. Only then did I finally understand the source of Sid's longstanding bitterness.

*Shirley Gould (above), born Sarah Goldman, Fall 1917
Sidney Goldman (left), Shirley's brother, 1915*

When I was a baby and Sid was five and a half years old, he caught scarlet fever, a dreaded disease before antibiotics. Quarantine, widely practiced at the time, was not an option. In Chicago, the Contagious Disease Hospital, which had just opened in 1917, was considered very scientific. And Mom, who put more trust in our non-Jewish family doctor's advice than in the folkways and superstitions that surrounded her, decided the hospital would be the best place for her sick son.

The Contagious Disease Hospital stay may have helped Sid recover from scarlet fever, but it must have been traumatic for him to be away from home. Worst of all for our relationship, Sid had been told that he had to go to the hospital because "if the baby gets it, it could kill her."

It was Christmas, and a big tree stood in the ward. The rigid nurse, who was said to be mean to the children, was very proud of this tree. Sid, who knew he was Jewish, refused to participate in any holiday festivities. My brother had to remain there a full twenty-eight days, with very few reminders of home. He did have a picture of me, his baby sister. That picture, now full of creases, rests in an old family album.

That was one of Chicago's snowiest winters, making it extremely difficult for anyone to visit Sid. Mom and my big brother Irv, then twelve years old, took three streetcars to get there, and when they walked from the streetcar stop, Irv had to walk in front of Mom to break a path through the snow. I found that part of the family story hard to believe until recently. During another big snowstorm, the huge snowfall of early 1918 was described in detail.

When I told Sid what I had discovered about the hospital, I felt the last trace of antagonism collapse. At that moment I began to see his chicken soup comment in a different light. Perhaps it hadn't really been an insult at all. Because it was apparent to Sid that I was trying to emulate our mother in every way, and because we all admired her achievements, perhaps he was simply expecting me to be as good as she was. I now consider his comment the highest compliment.

I've since cooked for and hosted many holiday meals, but that one remains my strongest holiday memory. From it I learned the important lesson that a person's intentions are not always what they seem. Right now, I'm looking forward to participating in Sid's ninetieth birthday celebration in California, where he lives. ●

Days of Awe

by Diane Turner

*T*he High Holidays have always felt like a mixed blessing. In past years, they represented a time to come together with friends and family, to set aside obligations and commitments to the outside world, and to contemplate the importance of endings and beginnings. The process has been joyful, inspiring, intellectually stimulating, and at times emotionally challenging. The fall of the year also has been a time of great difficulty. It is the season when I was diagnosed with melanoma and had surgery on my leg to remove a malignant mole. In the fall my daughter, Rebecca, was diagnosed with a rare seizure disorder, which shifted the course of our lives forever.

This year, *Yom Kippur* fell on a Thursday, just a few short weeks after the September 11th tragedy. Shock and horror stunned the world, and my husband, Robert, was dying of multiple myeloma, a bone marrow cancer. The doctors and nurses were telling us that his death could happen at any time. Robert had held his own until several days earlier.

To Jews, dying around or during the High Holy Days is very sacred. It is said that only the holiest and most righteous die at this time of year. Robert was an obstetrician/gynecologist, dedicated to bringing new life into the world; he took his calling very seriously and with great humility.

On *Yom Kippur* morning, knowing that our community would be praying together without us, I sat at home by Robert's bed, reading from the prayer book, talking about missing our friends and family, and knowing that next year, he would not be with us. In the afternoon, several close friends came to pray with Robert and me. We had all prayed together many times before, and it seemed appropriate to ask that Robert's soul travel into the light as the afternoon sun set. We stood around him, holding hands, as we surrounded him with our love. We prayed that he be released from his physical suffering, and we each expressed our love for him. At that moment, a great stillness came over the room. Robert's face looked peaceful, as if he understood and appreciated being sent off from this life. In the silence of this exquisite calm, everyone embraced for comfort, then left to return to the larger prayer community for *Yizkor* and *Neilah*. Although Robert's death did not occur for three more days, we felt a powerful release on a day when that is the primary intention—to be released.

Next year the High Holidays will certainly arrive with mixed feelings. Alone now, I will rejoin family and friends to acknowledge endings and beginnings. This time, I will be even more aware of the fading light on the afternoon of *Yom Kippur. Yizkor* and *Neilah* will always be a reminder of Robert and the light that he brought into my life and the lives of so many others. As the *Yom Kippur* rituals come to a close, I know that I, too, will be released from the many difficult times of past years but connected, always, to Robert. ●

Alone on Yom Kippur

by Elliot Zashin

*Y*ears before my *Bar Mitzvah,* I fasted on *Yom Kippur.* My parents spent most of the day in the synagogue, and my mother saw no reason to prepare any meals. Our house was quiet, and I felt lonely. I could have gone into the kitchen and helped myself to a snack, but I didn't. On *Yom Kippur* as an adult, I carried that sense of aloneness with me, even while observing rituals with other Jews.

This feeling struck me most forcefully the year I accepted an academic fellowship at the University of Southern California. Temporarily leaving behind my wife and two young sons, I departed for Los Angeles shortly before *Yom Kippur.* I felt the need to observe the holiday, but I didn't know any Jews in the city and hadn't yet been to the Hillel on the USC campus.

The rabbi-director was a young woman who understood how important it was to create rapport quickly among the worshippers, especially the new students and occasional attendees from the faculty and local community. Early in the service, she invited us to pair up with another person to share our expectations for that *Yom Kippur.* Sharing something personal with another individual, even a stranger, felt reassuring.

At times, the rabbi led the *davening* in English. That was a revelation. For once I knew exactly what I was saying during certain prayers.

But my first really spiritual moment came in the afternoon. We had reached the point in the service where, according to tradition, the High Priest prostrated himself before the Holy of Holies and confessed his sins, while the congregation awaited his return from this moment of total vulnerability. In my experience, the typical enactment was reserved for the rabbi and perhaps the cantor. In the past, the prostration had struck me as archaic and out of character for a modern rabbi. But now the rabbi invited us to join her, if we felt comfortable, in prostrating ourselves on the floor at the front of the small Hillel sanctuary. She explained that she meant not just kneeling or bowing, but total prostration with arms and legs spread out. The suggestion seemed a bit strange, but I felt drawn to accept the invitation. For the first time, I sensed dimly what *V'anachnu korim* really expressed.

As we progressed toward *Neilah,* I felt the lightness that sometimes comes from a long day without food. The sun was setting; the windows of the sanctuary were placed so that the last rays of the sun cast their diminishing light toward the Ark. As the shadows lengthened and darkened, I could almost make out the "closing gates." The small group of remaining worshippers chanted our final prayers in semi-darkness.

A break-the-fast lifted the hushed mood. I ate a little, but my feeling of being a stranger returned as I saw people embracing each other and exchanging one last wish for a good year. I drove back to my temporary lodging, feeling alone once more but no longer quite so lonely.

The next day I would meet my new colleagues at the School of Religion. I would start looking for my own apartment. And, I would definitely return to the Hillel. It was a new year. ●

Plotz and Pans

by Jeff Balch

*A*t eleven years old Soozers was still pretty spry, and she disappeared upon arriving at the cousins' house for the *Yom Kippur* break-fast. She knew the house, and she was the kind of pooch who looked after herself. So nobody noticed she was missing until close to dessert time. Then she was located in a backroom corner where an eighteen-ounce package of Oreos had been. She was on her side with eyes closed, breathing shallowly, next to a package containing a single Oreo. She had weighed twelve pounds when she arrived. Now, packed with Oreos, she weighed a little over thirteen.

What must have been her thoughts as the last Oreo lay before her, uneaten?

She was sick for many hours. With a little coaching she learned to heave into a pan. She recovered by the end of the next day.

A few months later, heading to the same house, we were on the lookout for signs of post-traumatic stress. We talked to her as we arrived. "It'll be okay Sooz," we murmured. "We'll keep an eye on you." She was frisking as we put her down inside the front door. She gave us a look, then headed eagerly to the infamous corner. It had been the site of her greatest agony, but also her greatest triumph. ●

Ruth and Dewey Gilbert, c. 1970s

In the Seventh Month on the Tenth Day

by Ruth Gilbert

*T*he year was 1961 and we were newlyweds. Even though my husband, Dewey, had been raised in a traditionally Jewish home and I am a Holocaust survivor, our own observance of Jewish holidays and rituals was nonexistent.

That year on *Kol Nidre* night we were entertaining my out-of-town cousin, who could spend only this one evening with us. We took him to dinner at a popular barbecue restaurant, and after we finished those finger-licking ribs, we decided to go somewhere else for dessert.

We all agreed on a German bakery and coffee shop in the area, a charming *gemütlich* place that served delicious pastries and coffee. It was frequented mainly by German nationals, and the language heard most often there was German. The bakery was packed on this *Kol Nidre* night and not with Jews. After waiting for quite some time to be seated, we finally got a table near the door. As we were perusing the menu, we suddenly felt a cold draft. The door had opened, and on the threshold stood a man. In those days we called this kind of person a bum; he was dirty and disheveled, his torn coat held together with safety pins. He carried two shopping bags filled with rags and junk. The man stood in the doorway for several minutes looking around the

room, then made a beeline to our table shouting, "Shalom."
He proceeded to talk to us in Yiddish, then turned around
towards the room and shouted, "Heil Hitler." Within minutes the
proprietor came over and escorted him out of the bakery.

Meanwhile, my husband and I sat frozen, staring at each other,
both wondering: Was this a messenger from God letting us know
we did not belong here on this of all nights? Was this Elijah
looking for us ? Or were we reading too much meaning into this
man's ravings? Whatever the reason, we both felt shaken to the
core. We quickly finished our dessert and left the restaurant.

My cousin did not seem affected by this encounter. And when
I asked him about it several years later, he didn't even remember
this happening. But neither my husband nor I ever forgot it.

Shortly after that evening, Dewey and I joined a synagogue.
And from then on, every *Kol Nidre* night found us at services. ●

"Home on the Range"

• •

by Ellen Kenemore

*W*hen my mother married into my dad's family, she must have felt as if she had entered a strange land, even though their families lived only a few miles apart. Her family lived in an apartment hotel off Lincoln Park with sweeping views of the lakefront. She came from a well-off family with Russian aristocratic roots, while my dad came from a much more modest Russian family. My mom attended the Reform congregation, Temple Sholom, which, when she was growing up, held its *Shabbat* services on Sunday mornings. Her grandmother's attitude was, "We're in America now, so we have to behave like Americans." My mother's parents exchanged Yiddish phrases with each other but not enough that it qualified as a second language for them.

In contrast, my dad's parents lived on the Northwest Side, had been Zionist union organizers with socialist leanings, sent their children to Yiddish school and kept kosher, but did not belong to a *shul.* And Yiddish was most definitely my dad's second language.

My parents often tell the story of Mom's first *Shabbat* dinner with Dad's family. According to them, my dad's mom, *Bubbie,* wanted to make sure my mom knew who they were and where they came from. To this end, the gathered family proudly sang every Yiddish song they knew. As the evening wound down,

Bubbie must have realized that my mother was feeling a little lost and felt empathy for her. *Bubbie* had herself first been an orphan and then an immigrant to this country at the age of twelve; she knew only too well what it felt like to be a stranger in a strange land.

So *Bubbie* suggested that everyone sing a song my mom would know, to help her feel more comfortable: "Home on the Range." All enthusiastically joined in, much to my mother's embarrassment.

"Why that song?" my mom wondered. It certainly had no particular meaning to her. But the choice made perfect sense to my dad. After all, it was President Roosevelt's favorite song and he was *Bubbie's* American hero, so it was *Bubbie's* favorite American song, too.

That is why at all my family's events, Yiddish songs are always translated—originally by *Bubbie* and later by my dad and aunt—and we always sing "Home on the Range." It has been fifteen years since *Bubbie* died, but we never miss an opportunity to remember her in this way. ●

My First Sukkot

by Betty Van Leuven

*T*here I was, on a muggy late September day, standing in the back room at Rosenblum's bookstore on Devon, waiting in line to pick up my *lulav* and *etrog*. I had converted to Judaism five years before and felt very comfortable doing the "big" holidays, but this was to be our first official *Sukkot*. I was determined to get it right.

I had done my homework. I knew the *lulav* is actually three different types of foliage, all of them symbolic—a palm tree branch combined with three boughs of leafy myrtle and two willow branches. The *etrog* is sweet-smelling and resembles a giant lemon. These items are intrinsic to the *Sukkot* ceremony. After a blessing is recited over them, they are waved in six different directions to remind us of the bounty and joy of the harvest season. I had thought to order ahead and was proud of my organized approach. I even had hours to spare before the time we had designated for the *sukkah*-building venture to begin in our backyard.

What I didn't understand was why I was the only female in sight and why all the black-hatted, bearded, and black-coated men were so intently scrutinizing the *etrogim*. They went from box to box peering at the yellow, wrinkled surfaces, turning each one end to end, then gently returning them to their mossy beds which reminded me of the fake grass my mother would use around the chocolate eggs and marshmallow bunnies to fluff out our Easter baskets. Pushing that image from my mind, I waited uncomfortably in my halter top and shorts, wishing my husband had volunteered for this particular errand.

Finally I reached the counter, behind which stood a sweaty man in a short-sleeved shirt. Unlike everyone else in the room, this man actually met my gaze.

"Goldberg," I said tentatively.

He gruffly barked, "Goldberg, what Goldberg? We got about ten a those."

Even more hesitant, I stammered, "L-L-Larry Goldberg."

To my immense relief, after a few moments of checking the corsage box look-alikes, he handed me one, as well as a long clutch of branches tied together. Ready to bolt like a scared rabbit, I felt him waiting for some further comment.

I mumbled, "Thank you."

Then he asked, "Well, what about your *s'chach*?"

I had never before come across that Hebrew word for the traditional evergreen branches used to cover a *sukkah* roof but sparsely enough to remain open to the sky. So I assumed the man was saying "shorts" with a Boston accent and was questioning my choice of clothing.

"Uh, sorry, I didn't realize there was a dress code," I murmured.

"No, no, how many bundles of *s'chach* did you order?"

I finally realized he could only be talking branches here and that I had ordered none. I quickly replied, "Oh, we got those already," and backed out with my treasures amid withering, sidelong glances. All the way home I chanted to myself, "Thank God for Jewish pluralism, thank God for JRC."

For our *s'chach,* we culled lovely-smelling evergreens from our own and neighbors' overgrown bushes. The *etrog* was perfect with its slightly lopsided shape and dimpled stem. We had a gaily decorated *sukkah,* as only a family with young children can conjure. The clear plastic that wrapped around three sides of our handmade frame blossomed with all manner of gaudy flowers whose paint ran in streaks with the first rain. And, I was grateful every day of that whole week for the opportunity to eat outdoors and gaze at the nighttime sky. ●

Stan Cohn with his daughter, Rachel, Sukkot 1996

Notes of a Sukkah-Builder

by Stan Cohn

*E*veryone has a special moment that marks the beginning of the Jewish New Year. It might be the apples and honey during a family meal at *Rosh Hashanah,* the striking solemnity of prayers during *Kol Nidre* and *Yom Kippur,* or the blast of the shofar at the end of *Neilah.* Over the last few years, my own new year moment has been the building of the *sukkah.*

For the past ten years we have built a *sukkah* on our back porch. Even though the materials are the same each year, somehow each *sukkah* carries its own special meaning. Over the years I have learned to listen to each *sukkah* and try to hear what it has to say. And, I have discovered several things.

Our *sukkah* is not fancy; I call it minimalist. It has no metal, no vinyl, no nails—just some thin wood planks lashed together with twine in a frame. It is open on all four sides. If we try to cover one of the sides of our *sukkah* with too much material, it catches the wind, bends, and sways; the more we leave the sides open, the steadier the *sukkah* stands. From this I have learned that the more we open our lives to our family, our friends, and the world around us, the more centered and stable our own lives will be.

On occasion we have put extra timber and evergreens on our roof, causing the *sukkah* to bow inward or lean precariously to one side. If we remove some of the excess *s'chach* and timber from the top, the *sukkah* once more becomes steady. From this I have learned that if we remove some of the unnecessary pressures from our lives—if we simplify and relax a little—we may find ourselves able to stand more fully upright, enjoying the world around us.

I also find that when I use very thick twine, which seems stronger, the *sukkah* ends up being less stable and more rickety. When I use smaller twine, I can lash the boards a little tighter, and the *sukkah* is better able to remain intact. From this I have learned that a number of small deeds done patiently can often bring about better results than trying to accomplish things with a single large gesture.

Each year I buy a few new boards and discard a few of the most weathered ones. Each year we make new decorations and discard those that can no longer withstand the wind and the rain. This reminds me that, like the *sukkah,* our lives always include loss and renewal. Our family, our friends, and all our past influences have helped shape our lives; we remember the lessons of those we have lost, and we treasure lessons learned from the new friends we meet.

Each year I enjoy *Sukkot* more, celebrating it in a *sukkah* filled with renewed hopes for a year of richness and beauty, joy and laughter. May each of you find your own messages in the joy of *Sukkot.* ●

By Any Other Name

by Judy Holstein

*E*ach fall I feel drawn to help build our congregation's *sukkah*. I like to participate with the other volunteers to create a structure which offers a welcoming environment and beckons people to gather in fellowship. Besides, this annual activity of building renews my connection to a holiday that has been special to me from birth.

I was born in 1946 on the first day of *Sukkot*. My parents told me over and over how much they enjoyed this happy coincidence. "A double reason to give thanks," they explained. To underscore the importance, they chose my name: "Suki."

So why am I called Judy? As soon as my parents announced my name, they received a barrage of warnings from friends: A little brown-haired girl in the U.S. in 1946 called "Suki"? They worried that such a Japanese-sounding name could evoke prejudicial treatment because of the post-World War II political sentiments in our country.

My parents succumbed to the pressure of such logic. For my new name they chose the biblical Judith. But my middle name "Sue" kept my connection to *Sukkot*. So, I go through life as Judy Sue, an all-American-sounding name that always reminds me of the holiday that welcomed me into life. ●

Family of Pat Lane, Lake Mills, Wisconsin, July 4, 1951

How to Build a Women's Sukkah

by Cynthia Lerner

*M*y friend Joanne and I are totally responsible for the observance of Judaism in our families. We each create a home environment for every Jewish holy day and holiday. In 1988, after five years of having *Pesach Sedarim* together, Joanne and I decided to make yet one more Jewish holiday a real part of our lives. Over dinner one summer evening, we announced to our husbands that we wanted to build a *sukkah,* in ritual celebration of the fall harvest. As usual, our husbands were willing to go along with the idea as long as they didn't have to do anything. So it would be a women's *sukkah,* untouched by male hands. We decided that the location of the *sukkah* would alternate between our two houses; this first year it would be at Joanne's.

Together and separately, Joanne and I researched the holiday in *The Jewish Catalogue* and Blu Greenberg's book, *How to Run a Traditional Jewish Household.* We spent hours looking through cookbooks, discussing who would cook what, whom to invite to dinner each night, and which nights we would accept invitations to eat in other people's *sukkot.* Would I be hurt if Joanne accepted an invitation to go somewhere else? Would I feel comfortable having company in the *sukkah* at Joanne's if she weren't there? We answered these questions with the wisdom of Solomon and were finally ready to actually build the *sukkah.*

"Why not?" we asked. "We're competent, how hard can it be? No 'easy-to-put-together' prefabricated *sukkah* for us!"

We drew the design on a piece of paper, a perfect square, ten feet each side. We figured we would need twelve pipes for the frame, strips of wood to lay across the top, and *s'chach*—evergreen branches—to place on top of the wood so that the sky and stars would be visible from inside the *sukkah.* Several days before construction was to begin at Joanne's, her husband asked how the pipes would fit together. In the *JUF News* we found an answer: connectors (designed for a prefabricated *sukkah*) that could be snapped onto the ends of the one-inch pipes we had purchased. We could buy the connectors we needed to hold our *sukkah* together, at a price that could easily have bought an entire prefabricated *sukkah.*

The Sunday between *Yom Kippur* and *Erev Sukkot* was a beautiful day. Joanne and I began building the *sukkah* while our husbands played their regular Sunday basketball game. Our sons, Mark, Josh, and Sam, made paper chains and pictures to decorate the *sukkah.* We soon realized that, even standing on ladders, we were not tall enough to fit the top pipes together. When our husbands returned, we requested their assistance. After some mild teasing about our women's *sukkah* needing a man's touch, Joe and Paul took turns climbing the ladder to attach the top of the frame and place the wood strips and the *s'chach* on top.

In spite of the weather taking a turn for the worse, we enjoyed every day of *Sukkot.* Toward the end of the holiday, my in-laws came to spend some time with their grandchildren. Upon seeing the *sukkah,* Herb and Evelyn had two questions: Why eat outside in the cold *sukkah* when we could eat inside where it's nice and warm? And why is it so tall? Joshua explained that in the desert thousands of years ago, the Jews had lived in temporary dwellings, so we eat in the *sukkah* for one week to commemorate our ancestors. Herb offered to cut the ten-foot-tall pipes down to seven feet. Since we insisted on having a *sukkah,* he explained, we should be able to put it together ourselves in the future. The next day, working alone, he spent eight hours cutting the pipes, helping to make our women's *sukkah* a lasting tradition.

Every year since then, around *Rosh Hashanah,* Joanne calls and asks if I'm ready to think about *Sukkot*—whom to invite and which nights we might go elsewhere. I love the idea of our sharing the *sukkah* each year, but it is Joanne who enjoys the actual building and eating in the *sukkah.* She will push and encourage me, and in turn, I will push and encourage my family to make the paper chains and help with the physical construction. No matter the weather, Joanne wants to eat in the *sukkah;* I am more hesitant when the weather is cold. For fourteen years we have built and dwelt in our *sukkah,* even through rainy, cold nights. We remember coming inside after eating dinner in the *sukkah* to watch the Dukakis-Bush Presidential debates. We remember when my daughter, Rachel, was born, welcoming her to the *sukkah* for the first time. We remember the first year Joanne's son, Mark, was at college in Boston instead of in the *sukkah* with us. We remember moving to Skokie and, finally, living only two blocks apart.

This year, Joanne won't be in Skokie for *Sukkot.* She is moving to North Carolina shortly after *Pesach.* I worry that without her here, it will be too difficult to build the *sukkah.* It is something that has always been ours, not mine. So this year, as I rebuild our *sukkah* for the fifteenth time, I will begin to build a new tradition, transforming our women's *sukkah* into my own. ●

Ray Grossman with his daughter, Aryn, and son-in-law,
Ted Froum, Detroit Marathon, Columbus Day 2000

Our Daughter's Intuition

by Darlene Grossman

*T*he time had come to make a decision: Would we retain the modest lifestyle to which we had become accustomed? Or would we suddenly become poverty-stricken?

Our oldest child was looking at colleges. I had always pictured her at my alma mater, a large, public, reasonably priced Midwestern university to which she had been offered a full scholarship.

Aryn, however, was eyeing a small, private, Jewish, obscenely priced, East coast, liberal arts university. She held both acceptance letters as we deliberated around the kitchen table. The vote was three (she, her father, and my wise friend) to one (me) in favor of poverty.

"All right," I said, playing the sanity card. "Before we lay any money on the line, you'd better take a look at the school to see if it's what you really want."

On a Friday several weeks later, Aryn boarded a plane for Boston, anxiously anticipating her first look at Brandeis University during their Prospective Student Weekend.

That Sunday evening we meet her at the airport. Hugs and smiles. Toss the duffel in the trunk. Pile into the car. Head home, holding my breath.

"So?" I finally ask.

"So," she replies. "I arrived Friday afternoon, met the freshman I was paired with, attended some classes, and spent the night in the dorm. Saturday I got the tour of the campus, met some faculty advisors, and spoke with some other students. I was asking myself whether this place was really worth the extra expense and the burden it would place on you. At that point, I had pretty much decided it wasn't."

My eyes widen. I dare to be hopeful. There is a God, I think, and She understands me. Our daughter will stay in Illinois; she'll be just a few hours away; I'll visit only when I'm called. We'll be able to afford an occasional roast on Shabbat.

"Saturday night," Aryn continues, "we all went to Chumley's, the campus coffee shop, and listened to the student improv group. They were fantastic, but I kept asking myself, 'Is this *really* worth it?'"

Oh, yes! I think contentedly. I'll bake her cookies and come visit on Mom's Day. I'll go to the art museum and watch Chief Illiniwek perform during halftime, just like when I was a student. Maris and Seth, our other children, will get new gym uniforms and new gym shoes. Things will stay status quo. Isn't life swell?

"Then, during the audience participation," Aryn goes on, "they asked for the names of people and places and body parts. You know the routine."

Yeah, yeah, I nod, lulled. I'm feeling secure in having trusted her judgment and am delighting in her story.

"Finally," she says, smiling back at me, "they asked for the name of a holiday. And a voice from the back shouts out *'Shemini Atzeret!'*"

"Where else in America," she wonders laughingly, "would a college student shout out *'Shemini Atzeret'*? And I knew I had found my school." ●

To Dance with Torah

by Bryna Cytrynbaum

*T*he year is 1991, the date October 16th, the holiday *Simchat Torah,* and the synagogue administrator is me. *Simchat Torah* at JRC is a congregant's delight and an administrator's nightmare. But little did I know that this holiday would open up my life.

In 1991, my fifth year as JRC's Executive Director, I asked myself, "What is it about *Simchat Torah* that causes me to tremble and have sleepless nights?" To begin, over two hundred chairs need to be removed from the sanctuary. Since JRC has no gigantic forklift for furniture removal, a small wagon must serve to cart four or five chairs at a time to the library, the hallways, the basement, and my office. All this so that JRC congregants can stand in a large circle around the sanctuary. All this so that they can unroll the *Torah* around the inside circumference of the human circle, each adult responsible for holding a piece of the precious parchment. Meanwhile, all the children congregate within this circle of *Torah,* after being warned against crashing into it and turning their small flags into daggers.

My first year here, I watched this unrolling, spellbound. My second and third years, I stood guard over two hundred taffy apples in the social hall. My fourth year, I patrolled the halls and bathrooms to remind would-be fencers and swordsmen that the flags were not meant for dueling or for stirring toilet bowls. But this year, my fifth year, 1991, promised liberation. Four hundred taffy apples were safely locked in the social hall and two custodians guarded the halls and washrooms. So for the first time, I was free to join the winding human chain, to enjoy the tumult and to dance with a borrowed tambourine.

The drama was ending, the *Torah* being rerolled, when suddenly Dale Good, a board member, asked if I would hold the *Torah.* I blurted out, "I've never done this before!" But I found myself already wondering how it would feel.

My mind raced backwards in time. I came from an Orthodox home, the daughter of a kosher butcher. I had never had the option of becoming a *Bat Mitzvah.* As a young adult, searching for my own identity as a Jew, I had asked my father, "Dad, in all the years you taught *Torah* to my brothers, as well as to other children, why didn't you teach me? I see that many Orthodox women today study together—admittedly separate from the men—but they do study *Torah.* So why didn't you teach me?" He took his time, and when he answered, he seemed sad. He simply said, "I didn't think about it." He had grown up in Europe, surrounded by his brothers, had studied in *yeshivot,* and had had no experience with girls learning.

But now I was about to hold JRC's largest and heaviest *Torah.* Dale whispered that I should cradle it in my arms, and if it got too heavy, I could pass it on to someone else. I eagerly reached out for the *Torah.* To my amazement, it wasn't heavy at all. Our Klezmer band, Heavy Shtetl, began playing, and the entire congregation started dancing in circles around me. I began dancing, too, nodding to everyone, as I moved with this treasure in my arms. I didn't want it to end. It felt so natural, I remember thinking, why haven't I done this before? Why hadn't I?

After *Simchat Torah,* I began thinking about other women at JRC who had studied to become *B'not Mitzvah.* Why not me? I wondered. I checked the JRC calendar and found an available weekend a year away: Thanksgiving 1992. Perfect! Within a

Bryna Cytrynbaum, Kate Kinser, and Marie Davidson at Bryna's and Marie's B'not Mitzvah, November 1992

week, I confirmed the date and convinced my dear friend, Marie Davidson, that we should do this together. Myra Weiss, from the Dawn Schumann Institute, was teaching a Monday morning *Torah* study class for women. Marie and I signed up.

Marie hired Kate Kinser as her tutor; I would study with Rabbi Reuven Frankel. Thus we began to take hold of *Torah,* studying separately, but giggling like school girls when we compared the different *tropes* we were taught. Together, we struggled with our *d'vrei Torah,* practiced on the *bimah,* and shopped for *Bat Mitzvah* oufits. We felt nervous, but once invitations were mailed, we realized there was no turning back.

Family and friends gathered. The doors of the Ark opened, and this time the *Torah* was unrolled just enough to reveal our *parsha, Toldot,* the Jacob and Esau story of sibling rivalry and the wish for parental approval, a father's blessing.

Even if, from time to time, my chanting of *trope* strays from the true notes, I have finally found my Jewish voice. Thanks to my *Simchat Torah* celebration, I have given myself a gift. And, I believe my father would approve. ●

Bathsheba Rubin, sister of Rebecca Rubin, Simchat Torah c. 1953

Torah, Torah, Torah

• •

by Raymon A. Grossman

*Y*ears ago, members of my synagogue routinely led holiday services for about twenty elderly Jews at a nearby nursing home. The service leader and a few others would conduct the service. Occasionally, one or two of the residents would read or sing a prayer. The others would sit there, not moving, in wheelchairs or on couches or chairs. They would lean and stare, mostly away from the leader or out the window, off in their own worlds. I often wondered whether these services really had any meaning for the residents.

Then I was asked to lead for *Simchat Torah.* As the day grew near, I realized that I would need a *Torah.* Usually we conducted these services reading from a *Chumash,* a bound copy of the *Torah,* but on *Simchat Torah,* tradition requires walking around the room with an actual *Torah* scroll.

I spoke to our rabbi. The synagogue had no extra scrolls, but he said he would loan me his old chaplain's kit from the Army. This big suitcase contained candles, candle holders, *kippot,* a *tallis,* prayer books, *dreidels,* a *challah* cover, and a little *Torah* scroll in an old cover.

Now I was ready. A few friends came along to keep me on key, to read responsively, and to assist any resident who should need help following the service or participating. The service began with me leading and my friends responding. We heard some snoring but noticed virtually no movement from the residents.

After about forty-five minutes it was time for the *hakafa,* walking around the room in a procession with the *Torah.* I picked up the little *Torah* with the old cover and began to march around. It was as if angels had come into the room. The unmoving bodies came alive. Hands reached for the miniature scroll, and voices never before heard in these services began to murmur; some became vibrant, joining in old familiar melodies. People we had never seen move before stood up to kiss the *Torah.* When we were done with the procession, the old people sat still and quiet again until they were led back to their rooms.

That day I experienced the presence of God more intensely than ever before in my life. I saw that young, passionate hearts can keep beating, even inside bodies that no longer seem alive. That was also the day I realized that I would never have sufficient words to explain what the *Torah* is. ●

Holy Sabbath

by Laura Friedlander

Kosher chicken
tastes better,
especially coated with crushed cornflakes;
and brisket oozes with dark juices—
the blood of our ancestors;
and the green beans are good for us.
Grandma makes true Thousand Island dressing
for her garden's pickle cucumbers and
fire-red tomatoes, all the while dreaming
of the thousand islands Papa Sam promised.
Aunt Syl's *matzo*-ball chicken soup is
the best, not only in Chicago,
but the Whole Wide World.
After supper
the ladies
use the sink,
still afraid of their dishwasher.
And now that I am old enough
to remember
I remember to help.
The water boils for tea.

The *mondel bread*
looks like Jerusalem stone,
and Syl's chocolate cake
like the earthworm's home,
rich and comforting.
There is candy
to satisfy the sweetest tooth:
bowls bloated with
tootsie rolls, chocolate-covered raisins,
watermelon sucking candy.
And when the feast is put on hold
until next Friday,
my brother and I
stumble pregnant
to the couch
for naps. ●

A Texas Thanksgiving

by Jonathan Markowitz

*T*o understand a Texas Thanksgiving, you have to understand that most Texans consider Texas the greatest state in the Union. In grammar school while kids in other states sing "God Bless America" and "The Star Spangled Banner," Texas kids sing, or shout, "Deep in the Heart of Texas" and "The Eyes of Texas Are Upon You." In Texas there is only one sport, Football with a capital F, and one football team, the Dallas Cowboys. I have heard relatives say, and mean it, that God made Texas Stadium with a roof open to the sky so He could watch His team play on Sundays.

I grew up in Dallas, a football-loving Texan whose favorite holiday was Thanksgiving. Not your regular, stuff-yourself-with-turkey-pumpkin-pie-and-all-the-trimmings Thanksgiving. No, a Texas Thanksgiving, a Texas Football Thanksgiving, a Dallas Cowboys Thanksgiving with all the trimmings.

My dad, my brother and I regularly attended, watched, and screamed together at Cowboys games; but the Thanksgiving Day Game is no ordinary game. Tension begins building a week or two into November when we start discussing whatever team will play Dallas for this Big Game. The Cowboys had struck a deal with the NFL that allows them always to play on Thanksgiving Day. The question is not if Dallas would play but when. Will Dallas have the less desirable 11:30 A.M. kickoff time, which does not mesh with the Thanksgiving meal, or the much better, mouth-watering 3 P.M. time slot? I scour the sports pages looking for the answer. After this official announcement, the call goes out to all the relatives: Game time is 3 P.M.; to get a good seat in front of the TV, get here half an hour before kickoff and, oh, by the way, check in with Mom to see what you're bringing.

Not that the food responsibilities ever change. Aunt Jean and her brood, old family friends from England, are always responsible for eight to twelve pies including pumpkin, pecan, traditional English Christmas pudding with the coins inside, and apple-mincemeat. We always make a turkey (at least a twenty-five pounder), stuffing, and the soup. My Uncle Buddy and his family bring a second twenty-five pound turkey, the potatoes, and vegetables.

My mom always invites people who have no family in the area. In Dallas if you are from out-of-state, you are indeed alone on this most important holiday. Non-family guests bring whatever my mom thinks they can manage but mostly salad or wine.

We start Thanksgiving Day by rearranging the house, emptying the playroom and setting up enough tables rented from Ducky Bob's to seat thirty to forty people. Begrudgingly we *schlep* every chair in the house into the playroom and place them around the tables. Next, with reverence befitting the High Holidays, we move around the furniture in our TV room to allow maximum game viewing without distractions from nonbelievers. Half an hour before game time I claim my spot, the Barcalounger close to the TV. My dad takes his traditional seat on the sofa, which affords the best view of the game. Everyone knows that seat is my dad's, his sole property, like Archie Bunker's chair, and no one would dare sit there during the game. Guests fill the other spaces. Kids come and go in little waves that look like drill team routines.

Jonathan Markowitz, far right, with his siblings and father, 1965

Occasionally they fight over seats and viewing angles, and adults referee to restore order.

Kickoff. A reverential hush fills the room. But after the kickoff return, unceasing banter breaks out.

"The game is fixed! Did you see that bogus penalty?"

"My God, Tom Landry [Dallas' coach legendary for his stoic nature and bad hat] is a *#&@·#*!"

"The Cowboys look great!"

"The Cowboys always flop on national TV."

Yada yada yada.

The Appetizer

The second quarter opens with the much anticipated Markowitz clam chowder. During the lengthy commercials, we all rush into the kitchen and fill our Texas-size, eighteen-ounce styrofoam cups. In short order, we wolf down the steaming Manhattan chowder, chunky with potatoes, carrots, zucchini, and, of course, minced clams fresh from their cans.

The Meal

My dad kicks off the next big foodball event, the two-minute warning, by screaming, "Leeenooore, two minutes!" We snap into action. My uncle, who always carves the turkeys during the first quarter, checks to make sure all the meat is off the bone. My mom, acting like a head coach, yells instructions at the kids. The kids, noisy and ignoring the instructions, hop to in their most annoying, deliberately slow manner. Like the Stanford Marching Band—who without any fixed marching pattern run haphazardly all over the football field, forming a pattern just in time—the kids set the table. Then tweet, the referee blows his whistle to signal both the end of the first half and our stampede to the glorious Thanksgiving dinner. We fill our disposable plates and carry them, sagging with turkey, mashed potatoes, stuffing, gravy, candied yams, green beans, and salad to the playroom. Excited over the Cowboys' first half, we loudly anticipate, with even more excitement, how this second half will bring Dallas a sure victory.

Dessert

The end of halftime thankfully signals the meal's end. We sluggishly march into the kitchen, toss our plates, and return to the TV room to watch the remainder of the game. It is now a struggle to remain interested, even though Dallas is winning; it is a struggle just to stay awake. Banter resumes, but mostly we are just waiting for the final whistle to signal Aunt Jean's pies. By the

Aunt Jean and her Pie Crew with Jonathan's mother,
Lenore Markowitz (right), Thanksgiving 2000

middle of the fourth quarter, I lose all interest in the game and begin to daydream about those legendary pies with their mounds of whipped cream.

At game's end, families and guests scrimmage over the desserts. As in football, everyone has his or her own strategy. My strategy: "flood the zone"—take a small piece of each pie to be sure to get all the textures and tastes. The kids' favorite strategy: "the rush"—run up as fast as you can, take a big piece of your favorite pie, then wait to go back for seconds. Some adults prefer "the blitz"—take two plates and two pieces, pretending to be getting some for another person as well.

After everyone eats their fill and the adults say how good all the food was, my mom gives her head coach signal for us to clean off the tables, put away the chairs (which don't actually make it back to their correct places for weeks), and fold up the rented tables for Ducky Bob's to pick up tomorrow. By 9 P.M. the guests are gone, all of them a little rounder and more content than when they came. The football game, centerpiece of Thanksgiving, begins to fade, and I resolve that next year I will try to balance football with a little less gluttony. ●

Thanksgiving in Grinnell

by Lesley Williams

For most of us, Thanksgiving evokes family memories: Moms and grandmas huddled over turkey stuffing, dads and uncles howling epithets at the TV, unsupervised younger cousins racing madly through the house until the tryptophan kicks in. Sweetly familiar and comforting, they reassure us of stability in a world gone mad.

So the first major holiday celebrated away from home is always a shock. Familiar rituals sacred as the High Holidays liturgy are revealed for the quaint family eccentricities they are. Friendships that have weathered bacchanalian excess and dubious hygiene founder over the amount of milk in the mashed potatoes and whether that ringed, wobbly red jelly counts as proper cranberry sauce.

Yet tolerance for others, no matter how bad their taste in condiments, is what the college experience is all about. Never was this clearer than during my freshman Thanksgiving at Grinnell College, in Grinnell, Iowa, population six thousand, including six black families, one Catholic church, and exactly zero Hispanics, Jews, or Asians. In Grinnell, being Italian qualifies as exotic.

In the town, that is. The student body was a great deal more eclectic, drawn from across the country to this "Harvard of the

Midwest." My freshman dormmates were a mixed bag. Teri, Stuart, Jeff, and Susan were all Jews from the East Coast. Vidya had grown up partly in Des Moines and partly in her parents' hometown in northern India. Edna was a Presbyterian minister's daughter from Virginia. Kouchiar, from Iran, was a refugee whose father had run afoul of the Shah. There was Mike, a born-again Christian from Montana. And me, the Chicago South-sider, eager to blend in and inordinately proud of my reputation as the black kid who got along with everybody.

Grinnell doesn't have a Thanksgiving break, so most of us were spending the holiday on campus that year, away from home for the first time ever. And Kouchiar had never before celebrated an American Thanksgiving, having arrived in the States less than a year earlier.

"Let's cook Thanksgiving ourselves!" suggested Vidya one afternoon. "We can all bring stuff . . ."

"I have this great pumpkin bread recipe," Edna broke in.

"I can make sweet rolls," I offered, wondering if they would be up to my great-aunt's standards.

"Wait till you try the Thaler family garlic stuffing!" cried Teri.

Everyone agreed to participate, even the guys, once they ascertained that a TV would be available. We set to work. Of course Edna and Susan had conflicting standards on thawing readiness, and Jeff's mashed potatoes resembled a gallon of Rocky Road, but we were getting there.

Kouchiar looked dubious. "What's all this gunk inside?" he asked, indicating the protruding guts of The Bird. As Teri explained the niceties of stuffing, he looked a bit green. Stuart kindly led him away to the TV (Bears 3, Lions 10) and introduced him to the traditional male Thanksgiving bonding prelude.

At last the meal was ready. The table gleamed with the finest Chinette, and the serving dishes groaned with turkey, Teri's stuffing, my rolls, Edna's pumpkin bread, Stuart's green beans, Jeff's potatoes, Mike's salad, Kouchiar's rice, and Susan's apple pie. We took our places at the table, filled with holiday excitement, camaraderie, and the thrill of our first Thanksgiving away from home. Before anyone thought to dissuade him, Mike stretched out his hands over the table, eyes closed, and intoned, "Lord Jesus, thank you for this food and this company. Thank you for giving us the chance to share your love among friends. Let this feast remind us of you, our one true Savior and King, and of your precious blood spilled for our sins. In Jesus' name, we say, Amen."

There was a stunned silence, as Mike opened his eyes to a sea of tight-lipped, angry faces. I saw Jeff and Teri exchange glances, Vidya twist her napkin, and Stuart drum his fingers nervously on the table and look away. The moment might have passed, we might all have swallowed our annoyance, but then . . .

"How dare you!" Enraged, Susan spat the words at Mike. "What kind of crap was that?!"

Mike blinked, uncomprehending. "I beg your pardon?"

She could barely choke out her retort. "You damn well should. Did it ever occur to you that some of us at this table are not Christian? That we really don't want to hear all this Jesus crap at our Thanksgiving dinner?"

The rest of us shifted uncomfortably in our seats, as Susan articulated emotions we had been too polite, or too cowardly, to express. This was not the warm, convivial Thanksgiving we had anticipated.

Mike favored Susan with a withering look of condescension. "I was just trying to bring in a little godliness. I'm sorry if 'God' offends your sensibilities."

"No, Mike," Teri said quietly. "'God' doesn't offend us. But praying about Jesus in a mixed group was pretty insensitive, don't you think?"

"Oh right, I'm the insensitive one. What about her? Calling Jesus 'crap' isn't insensitive?" Mike was near tears. "You people better pray that *He* can forgive you, 'cause I sure can't." And with that he stormed out. A stifling silence descended, and everyone glared at Susan. Quietly, Jeff eased out of his chair and went looking for Mike, who, mollified, returned to the meal with an air of injured magnanimity. Somehow, we finished that dinner in civility, if not peace. I was crushed: How could things have gone so wrong? How could Mike be so arrogant about his Christianity, and how could the others be so accepting? As it happened, they thought Susan should apologize to him!

"Well, she did kind of ruin the party, " whispered Vidya as we washed the dishes. "She did insult him."

I was stunned. "Didn't you feel insulted by Mike?" I asked.

She sighed, "Well, sure. But he didn't mean any harm. He probably didn't know any better."

I snorted. "He does now."

"But she didn't have to make such a big deal about it," said Vidya, exasperated. "Why couldn't she just let it go, like everyone else?"

How many times had I heard this same complaint about Susan: "Why won't she just let it go? Why make such a big deal out of it?" While other Jews and non-Christians sighed, swallowed, and looked away, Susan took action. When the director of her secular choir decided to perform *The Messiah* for a holiday concert, Susan wore huge *Magen David* earrings to every performance. When our dorm social coordinator planned a "nondenominational" December study party, featuring Secret Santas, tree-shaped cookies, and carol singing, Susan posted the invitation on the communal bulletin board and wrote at the top, "How is this 'nondenominational'?"

Stubborn as Mordecai, uncompromising as Daniel, Susan saw

the world through the eyes of an outsider, the perennial thorn pricking those who preferred the comfort of accommodation to the struggle of being different. Jews and non-Jews alike accused her of being stubborn, uncompromising, a troublemaker. I cringed more than once when called on to defend her actions. But defend them I did, because deep down I agreed with her.

But that weighty realization was still far away on that Thanksgiving afternoon. I slouched down beside Kouchiar on the couch (Bears 6, Lions 28). He slung his arm around me and grinned. "Typical Thanksgiving, eh?"

I grunted. "Not exactly."

"Come on," he said. "Every family party I've ever been to ended just like this. Someone says something stupid, someone else yells, and someone storms out. Then we eat."

"But this was supposed to be different. All of us together, sharing family recipes and traditions."

Kouchiar laughed. "You Americans. Always wanting to 'share' and 'try new experiences,' as long as it doesn't threaten what you're comfortable with."

And of course he was right. Being *comfortable* around others— what a sad, sorry goal that was.

I leaned against Kouchiar, who was still absorbed in the game. Maybe he was right. Maybe this was just the way Thanksgiving should be. And I dozed off on the couch, wondering where in Grinnell I could find Susan some chocolate *Chanukah gelt.* ●

The Cousins' Club Is Coming!
The Cousins' Club Is Coming!

by Eileen Heisler

*T*hink of a Cousins' Club as a High Holy Day—one that came regularly one Sunday each month. For those who haven't had the pleasure, a Cousins' Club was a holdover from our *Bubbies'* and *Zadies'* early days in America. It stemmed from a time when just a handful of relatives from their beloved *shtetl* had arrived in America, their newly adopted land.

Here these relatives struggled desperately to learn English and to prove they belonged by winning citizenship. But at Cousins' Club, they happily lapsed into the comforts of Yiddish.

As many as thirty cousins might attend, along with spouses and children. We met in the basements of those fortunate enough to have their own homes. Some lucky Sunday evenings, the cousins came to our own basement. No one thought of missing a meeting. Nor did anyone dare take an assignment lightly. Each family held its place in the hierarchy and worked hard to gain the others' respect.

We kids religiously accompanied our parents, *Bubbies,* and *Zadies* to monthly meetings. And these really were meetings, not just get-togethers. Cousins' Club meetings were as well regulated as ancient Jewish dietary laws and demanded as much regard as *Shabbos* itself. The Cousins' Club boasted elected officers, formal agendas, recorded minutes, dues collections, planned menus, project assignments, and arrangements for charitable donations.

Despite their order, the meetings were noisy affairs. This was the time to share news. Here we kids learned words like *greenhorn, shtetl,* and *treif.* We also overheard heated debates on whether to work, travel, or write on *Shabbos.* For this new world had little use for the *Shabbos* habits brought over from the *shtetl.* In contrast, life in 1950s Chicago was pure potential. All these newcomers had to do was recognize opportunity, allow themselves to move with its momentum, and turn aside from their old world ways.

As in the ongoing debates about *Shabbos* observance, the Cousins' Club meetings offered other evidence of the old world yielding to the new. For example, where did our cousin with the strong Yiddish accent get a name like Betty? And when did our complex last names become so simple, so monosyllabic? What fueled the cousins' intense interest and competition over whose children went to which university?

Families that left Chicago for suburbs like Skokie were considered pioneers, charting undeveloped territory without public transportation or familiar *shuls,* delis, or kosher butchers. And surely, the Chicago cousins speculated, such suburbs could never offer a comfort and familiarity to rival that of the Cousins' Club.

We children of the Cousins' Club have all managed to land in far-flung communities. Thanks to our sophisticated educations, we are successful and independent in occupations our *Bubbies* and *Zadies* would never even recognize. But what has become of that noisy, extended family support system that ushered newcomers from the old *shtetl* life into this American one? As children, we never imagined that the Cousins' Club could come to an end. And, as successful American adults, we still mourn its disappearance. ●

Babci's Christmas: A Memory

by Joan E. Dumser

During the years of negotiation prior to our marriage, the "Christmas Discussion" came up often. As a committed cultural Jew, my future husband saw a Christmas tree as the ultimate assimilation. Put up a tree and next you'd be eating Ritz crackers at the *Seder* table. The thing I miss: the smell of pine in the house. The things I don't miss: undecorating the tree and finding pine needles in the rug until May.

With the passage of time, as our years of Jewish family life grow in number, I think it should get easier. I think that the crisp air, a dark night, colorful lights shining in the neighborhoods should have no effect on me. I used to think that my feelings could all be neatly packed away, just like the dusty box of Christmas ornaments in my basement I still refuse to throw out.

But each year around the winter solstice, I get anxious, nostalgic, and cranky. Christmas is not on my calendar, and it often comes as a surprise to me, as if I've just spotted reindeer on the roof. Suddenly I'm struck with an urgent need for *pierogis*.

When I was little, we always spent Christmas Eve with my grandmother, or *Babci* (BAHB-chy), as we called her. She lived on the second floor of the two-flat we had all been born into on Chicago's Northwest side. In the Polish Catholic tradition, the day before Christmas is a fast day—no meat and light meals only. But as traditions change and grow, the dinner, known as *Vigelia* (Vi-GEE-liah), had evolved into a big feast. Although still meat-free, it was a grand event with a number of fish dishes that varied only slightly from year to year—sometimes the scalloped oysters my brother loved, and once in a great while a truly vile pickled eel dish that made the children squeal and run from the room. The guardians of the table remained herring, *pierogis,* and an exquisite homemade cream of mushroom soup, made only with imported dried Polish mushrooms. Each year a tiny packet of this black gold came from my aunt, who lived behind the Iron Curtain in Warsaw. How she got them out to us, and how my grandmother could make from them a pot of soup big enough for the whole family, remains a mystery.

But the most special treats were the hand-made *pierogis.* Nowadays you can buy something called *pierogis* in the grocery store any day of the week. But *Babci* made them only once or twice a year, sometimes at Easter, but always, always for Christmas Eve. And, as far as I knew, there were only two fillings, sauerkraut and mushroom, or cheese—the ones she said were for the children but were her favorites, too.

Pierogis resemble ravioli and *kreplach* only superficially. Yes, they are made of dough, and yes, they include a filling. But a perfect *pierogi* has the precisely correct proportion of dough to filling. The dough, like a piece of fine silk, is thin, almost translucent, and drapes over your hand like warm air. The filling is savory, not too salty, and the sauerkraut a bit tart. And then, of course, you must fry a *pierogi* in butter before serving. *Babci* lived to be ninety-six, telling us every day that a little butter wouldn't hurt.

Not counting the days of cooking, cleaning, tree-decorating, present-searching, and clothes-ironing, preparation for *Vigelia* began early on the morning of Christmas Eve. My mother would get us up to help in the process by insisting that sleeping late on this day meant bad luck for the year to come.

Zachary Rudin, son of Joan Dumser, lighting Chanukah candles, 1990

With our jobs done, the meal started with a thin wafer called *Opwatki* (Oh-PWAHT-ki). It looked like a communion wafer but came in rectangular sheets about the size of a post card. The elders in the family—*Babci,* Mom and Dad—each started with a full sheet, laid them on top of each other, and broke them so that each person came away with a piece of all three wafers. We moved and mingled around the table, repeating this exchange of wafers, kissing and hugging until each family member had received a broken piece from everyone else and had offered best wishes for the coming new year. You finished with only a few crumbs to call your own, and the carpet was covered in white specks of wafer.

Then the girls and women carried the food to the table: the hot soup splashing on the floor, the herring served with black rye bread, and the main course of fish. All the relatives sat crammed at the table, elbow to elbow, with barely enough room to pass the dishes. And the meal that had taken days to prepare always dragged on too slowly for the children, who knew that afterwards we'd be able to open the gifts waiting under the tree, but only those from *Babci.*

When my parents moved to the East Coast, their six adult children would still make the effort to get home to them at Christmas time. And with the collected spouses and offspring, we would make *Vigelia.* When our boys were very young, my husband and I still joined them all. Eventually, though, it seemed to make more sense for us to take the little vacation time we had together and go to Florida. There, I never feel the pull of the holiday; no matter how many lights you put on a palm tree, it will never look like Christmas to me.

I can still smell the dinner, hear the family voices, see the piles of dishes in the kitchen. All these years later, I remember the commotion, the joy, and the tension that filled the air. But Christmas is not mine any more. It belongs to the past.

My husband and I have not created a hybrid of Christmas-*Chanukah;* nor have we set down a fixed ritual. Each year we devise new rules for the season. How many presents will we give the boys? Will we hand them out all on one night or spread it out through the week? Is it bigger present to smaller or the other way around? Are gifts at *Chanukah* relevant at all? Are we borrowing too much of the Christmas tradition? But without a doubt, I know that if I make too much of it, searching for special little gifts, wrapping them up just so, it will feel too much like I'm getting into the Christmas spirit.

Each year as the days get shorter, I have the urge to pull out the good china and set the table for a feast. Some years I call it *Shabbat* dinner; sometimes the *pierogis* share the table with *latkes.* On every night of *Chanukah,* we set out all of the *Chanukiot,* from the children's hand-painted preschool efforts to the brass heirloom from my husband's family. We line them up on the dining room table and light them together. I don't think of what I have given up, but rather of the Jewish traditions we share as a family. As I light the *menorah* the irony is not lost on me: *Chanukah* is the holiday commemorating the Maccabees, who fought to preserve their identity. And so, I light the candles in memory of who I was. ●

Tinsel Time

●●●

by Rochelle M. Bernstein

As a reflective child of the '60's, I sat in, marched in, read in, spoke out at speak-ins, and hungered for relevance. While I didn't "turn on and tune in," I did "drop out" (of Temple University) to pursue relevance in the real world. I would (tah-dah!) go forth and change the system from within. After a few months of late-adolescent angst, I took the Civil Service exam and got a job with the Internal Revenue Service. Now there was a system!

Please note, I never said I wasn't naïve. Hopeful? Yes. Well-intentioned? Certainly. But I was greener than hydroponic turf and about as ready to stand up to heavy traffic. I'd been working for about eighteen months when several of my IRS colleagues asked me why I wore a small silver whistle around my neck all the time. I thought they were kidding and said the first thing that came into my mind: "I coach a girls' basketball team after work." When they started to ask me questions about the team and how the season was going, I quickly explained that I really didn't coach a team and briefly described the significance of my large silver *mezuzah*. After a silence that made the Bronze Age seem short, their eyes regained focus, and one woman finally said, "You mean (long pause), you're Jewish?!"

I grew up in one of five non-Catholic families (three Jewish, one Swedish Lutheran, and one Quaker) in a Lithuanian-Irish neighborhood in South Philadelphia. By the age of five, we'd identified the mysterious difference between Jews and Catholics: Jews ate fish on Thursday nights while Catholics ate fish on Fridays. I learned a lot about the dominant Christian culture. It hadn't occurred to me that most people in that culture knew very little about me, a Jew.

After the whistle episode, I was elected the local Guide to the Perplexed Gentile. I fielded such questions as

Why are Jews not Christians?

Why don't Jews believe in Jesus? (Yes, I thought I'd covered it, too.)

How are Jews not an obscure anti-Trinitarian sect vaguely related to Quakers or Unitarians?

Why don't Jews eat pork or shellfish? ("It's not kosher" I knew required appropriate biblical citations.)

Why don't you eat cheeseburgers? (The standard "Don't boil a kid in its mother's milk" explanation worked. Thank goodness I never had to deal with *shatnes.)*

By my third Christmas there, most IRS people I knew were wishing me Happy *Chanukah.* It had become a tradition that the Friday before Christmas our office took over a local restaurant for two hours and had an enormously good time. We would eat too much, partake of Christmas cheer in many liquid forms, and the bosses would laugh and sing carols like everyone else; then we would trudge dutifully back to our desks for the last hour of our 7 A.M. to 3 P.M. shift. I had assumed it was in deference to the principle of separation of church and state that we never decorated the office. So I was surprised when my boss called me over to say he'd chosen me and Lana Paris—the only two Jews in the unit—to shop for our Christmas decorations, including a mock Christmas tree.

A rival unit had sneaked in early one morning and mounted a fully decorated and tinseled tree on top of their file cabinets. Our instructions were to uphold the honor of the regiment, uh, unit. We took Lana's car, which had the bigger trunk, and off we went to brave the pre-Christmas crowds at Toys 'R Us.

After bumbling down several aisles lacking Christmas decorations, Lana saw the overhead signs, which led us to the trees. We rejected the silver, the metallic pink and blue, and the flocked varieties and settled on a green one. It looked like a tree from some unnatural landscape, but we could afford it, and it didn't require an engineering degree to assemble. We moved on to ornaments. First we considered sparkly, imported glass ones.

I remembered, as a child, finding a dozen glass Christmas balls in the detritus of my father's defunct grocery store. Every year he had hung them in a display window on a long garland as a gesture to his non-Jewish customers. To Bart Davis, Lowell Lipshultz, and me, the shiny glass balls morphed into hand grenades. We crouched behind the old freezer, pulled out the "pins" (wire hangers) with our teeth, and lobbed the grenades over an old sofa. They fell with a very satisfying pop, crash, tinkle-tinkle to wipe out the German machine gun nest. Then, of course, we charged over the sofa and took the hill. What a mess.

We decided against glass ornaments. Too dangerous. Besides, Lana noted that they all seemed to come from Communist-dominated countries, and we should not support Soviet oppression. Instead, we chose silky balls in several colors, sizes and textures. We zipped through lights and garlands. Then we hit the wall: tinsel.

I knew one thing about tinsel. Two schools of thought vied for dominance as diametrically opposed as the schools of *Hillel* and *Shammai.* The school of *Shammai* advocated distributing individual strands of tinsel evenly over the entire surface of the tree. *Hillel,* on the other hand, went for handfuls jubilantly tossed helter-skelter, and if amounts were limited, only on those parts of the tree that were most visible. But how much tinsel was enough? Like raisins in a *kugel,* could too much be bad?

Back at the office, co-workers with more Christmas tree experience took pity on us and recited the proper order for decorating a tree: lights, balls, garlands, tinsel. Our tinsel compromise was to place small handfuls of tinsel on strategic branches. We worked past the end of our shift to finish it all, including an aluminum foil *menorah* with multi-colored candles under the tree. Several maintenance guys from the second shift helped us lift the tree onto a table. We duct-taped the stand securely to a table top and left for the night.

The next morning the third unit put up its tree. Our gray cinder block building had turned quite festive. People smiled a little more than usual, exclaiming, "Wow!" and "Great job!" We felt encouraged. But "What's that aluminum foil thing under the tree?" quickly followed. We spent a lot of time telling the *Chanukah* story to everyone in the building.

Then I saw our crew looking from tree to tree. The first unit's tree sat resplendent in red and gold. The third unit's white, flocked tree was a merry red and green. Our tree had blue and white lights; blue, white, and silver balls and garlands; and (despite our raisin *kugel* philosophy) a little less tinsel than the others.

"The colors," someone finally offered. "They're not really Christmasy, are they?" I smiled as I remembered walking to school with Sherry Zucker and Edith Black. We listened in disbelief as Sherry described the tree and the lights her parents had put up in their apartment as *Chanukah* decorations. Edie and I just knew there was no such thing as a *Chanukah* bush. "Well," I admitted silently, "I guess I was wrong." After all, we had just given our IRS office a *Chanukah* bush for Christmas. ●

A Warm Chanukah

●●●

by Richard Shure

*I*n 1970 we were living on the Air Force base just outside of
Minot, North Dakota. I had applied to take the Professional
Engineers exam, which would be held in Bismarck. Since the
exam was a two-day affair—a written exam on Friday and an oral
exam on Saturday—I would need to spend at least one night in
Bismarck.

Feeling lonely Friday after the exam, I tried to call the temple
listed in the phone book, hoping they would have a Friday night
service. But no one answered. In the local paper I noticed the
picture of a child lighting a *Chanukiah,* so I looked up this family's
name in the phone book. When I called to inquire about services,
I learned that there was no longer a rabbi or formal services at the
temple. That evening, however, almost every Jew in Bismarck
would be at this family's home to celebrate *Chanukah.* I was
given directions and invited to come, too.

I don't know why it always surprises me that the cloth we
Jews are made of may be woven on many looms in different
parts of the world. But the tightness of the weave and its ability
to offer warmth must be universal. In the soft light of the
Chanukah candles, I saw that I was among family I had not yet
met. The dinner and services all felt familiar. Later, several people
savored telling me how their families had come to settle in

Rich and Alma Shure, Officers Training School, San Antonio, Texas, Winter 1967

Bismarck. One, for example, described a grandfather who made a living traveling by horse from small town to small town selling pins. In slow times, he had rubbed carbon to reblacken stoves.

When I left that evening, we exchanged names and phone numbers. My host family raided their freezer to retrieve bagels and lox, shipped from Minneapolis, to put together a care package for my wife, Alma. Before we left North Dakota, we traveled back to visit those Bismarck families. As before, we were made welcome and fed well.

Most winters, Bismarck gets cited at least once as the coldest spot in the nation. But I will never forget the warmth of that city's close-knit Jewish community. ●

The Eighth Night

by Isaac Bloom

*I*t was the last night of *Chanukah,* and the smell of eight burning candles mixed with the lingering scent of baked chicken, potatoes, onions, and the rest of the *Chanukah* feast. I was a young, energetic boy who had refused too many "go to beds" and was intent on staying up late, especially tonight. After all, it was the last night of the best holiday. My annoying parents had already ordered me to do the regular prebedtime chores— brushing my teeth, changing my clothes—you know the drill. I was just waiting for those telling words: "Isaac, sweetie, it's time for bed!"

This night is going to be different, I told myself; I'm gonna really put up a fight. I decided I would need more than my usual argument—studies done at Harvard say it is not good for you to get too much sleep and that, in fact, you'd be better off with less. This time I needed something new.

My idea had just started to form when I heard the words, "Isaac, honey, time for bed." Those two parents of mine had beaten me to it. But then, a loud bang and a screech from my cat came from the living room. I used this chance to investigate and get out of going to bed. I thought I was so smart. I had just eluded my parents' orders, thanks to my awesome cat. But when I looked around to thank him, a glow caught the corner of my eye. A flame that did not belong to the *Chanukah* candles anymore was licking the center of the table. I watched in horror as the flame grew in front of my eyes; it seemed a blazing inferno.

I forgot about my plans to skip bedtime and immediately ran to my parents. "Mom, Dad, the table's on fire!"

I expected my father to leap into action and save us all, but instead I got another, "Isaac, there is no fire, now go to bed!"

I even tried dragging them, but my parents would just not cooperate. I thought I was going to die! Using all of my strength, I tried once more: "You guys, would I lie about this? The table's on fire!"

"Jake, I think I'll just go check," my mom said. All of a sudden she screamed, "Holy S**t, Jake, the table's on fire!"

Quick as lightning, my dad grabbed a bucket of water and extinguished the blazing table.

After being thanked for saving us all, I actually was a little tired. I set the wet candles back into the *menorah,* moved them to a safe spot on the stove, sat down on the couch, and began to doze off. A little noise caught my attention, though; the culprit had returned. My cat quietly circled the table, surveying the damage he had caused. He caught me eyeing him and returned the stare.

When I woke up the next morning, with the *Chanukah tzuris* behind us, I looked at my surroundings. My room was still there, my sheets were still wrapped tightly around me, and I was safe. I told myself that I would never forget the smell of those eight melting candles mixed with the lingering scent of baked chicken, potatoes, and onions—now mixed with a little smoked oak. ●

The Light Went Out on Chanukah

by Susan Stone

Chanukah 1970.

There we were. Five of us on a cold December night. There had been six of us. The rectangular kitchen table held six chairs. We each had our favorite place. One chair was empty. We lit candles with no joy as my nineteen-year-old sister's funeral was just a week earlier. Car accident.

Everyone was steeped in deep grief. My parents, my little sister and brother. Me, home from graduate school. The phone call had come when I was alone in my apartment, studying. It was my dad. "What's wrong?!" I could tell by his voice something was horribly wrong. Was it my mom? Younger, healthy siblings don't die. Didn't cross my mind. Besides, why was he calling instead of my mother?

It was *Chanukah.* We sat around the table with no appetites. The doorbell rang. It was the *rebbetzin,* bearing a plate of *latkes. Latkes* for *Chanukah.*

Bearing a bit of thoughtfulness and love on a lonely, lonely *Chanukah* night when the candles cast their light but couldn't penetrate our hearts. Our hearts were dark. ●

Steven, Judy and Beth Salzman, children of Gerry Salzman, Chanukah 1966

For My Jewish Daughters

by Susan Cherry

*D*ecember arrives bedecked in bulbs
of every hue, pine and velvet around her neck,
a gaudy tiara of expectation
pinned into her frosted hair.

Awestruck by her dazzling mien,
you beg to have a baubled tree,
to sit on Santa's padded lap,
to carol dressed in green and red.

Your longing tramples on my heart
like reindeer feet, demanding to know
why I've chosen to deprive you
of the season's treats.

Perhaps some day you'll understand
I'm giving you Identity,
which hasn't the shimmer of tinsel and ribbon,
but lights a lifetime steadily. ●

Anna Berkson, daughter of Laura Friedlander and Adam Berkson, Chanukah 2000

Holiday Wake-up Call

by Jan Wishinsky

*I*n the late 1950s and early 1960s, my family lived in a subdivision outside Baltimore, Maryland, where almost every family was Jewish. While electric *Chanukiot* glowed in many windows, the sole Christmas decoration was one modest wreath. Each year, my parents packed us four kids into the old blue station wagon, so we could drive around town admiring the holiday lights in other neighborhoods. After seeing these wonders, I exclaimed, "Gee, I didn't realize there were so many Gentiles in the world!" ●

*Samuel and Vera Shulmeister, paternal grandparents of Nina Raskin,
with children Frances and Arnold, Omsk, Siberia, 1904*

Christmas-Chanukah: A Journey

by Nina Raskin

When I was little, I loved visiting Aunt Frances, my father's older sister by thirteen years. She and Uncle Jascha lived in an apartment in a converted brownstone on West 70th Street in Manhattan. In their tiny apartment, everything was on a small scale. The kitchen was the size of a closet, and the ice came up in the dumbwaiter. We listened to Caruso on a victrola with a picture of a little dog under the appellation: "His Master's Voice." We went there every Christmas.

On Christmas Eve, Uncle Jascha would search the neighborhood to find the tiniest, cheapest Christmas tree that remained. Aunt Frances would decorate it with tiny ornaments, tenderly sequestered from Omsk in Siberia, where her parents, my Grandma and Grandpa Schulmeister, had lived after secretly converting to Russian Orthodox Christianity.

One Christmas Day I particularly remember. I might have been five years old at that time. Uncle Jascha entertained us with charades, while Aunt Frances completed her elaborate and seemingly endless dinner preparations. Because the kitchen and dining area were so small, Aunt Frances refused any help. Finally, the Christmas dinner was ready, and the lights on the ragged little tree were turned on. First we had *pirozhki,* filled with meat, potatoes, kasha, or cabbage. Then there was a roast leg of lamb, mint jelly, Aunt Frances's prize-winning lentil-and-rice casserole, creamed mushrooms and onions, and finally, my Aunt Frances's noblest creation, orange cake. After this repast, my cousins and I lounged on the daybed couch while mysterious preparations took place.

When the doorbell rang, we all ran to see who was there. Santa Claus, with a definite Slavic accent, greeted us with a pack of presents slung over his back. I was dazzled and honored that Santa could find us on the second floor of my Aunt and Uncle's walk-up apartment. But something strange happened after the presents were distributed. "Santa is losing weight," said my Aunt Frances as she extracted a pillow from Santa's fine red suit. I pondered this development over the next year, and by the following Christmas, I had figured out that Santa Claus was my Uncle Jascha.

That same winter my parents brought me to my Grandma King's house to spend a day or so visiting with my cousin Carol. Grandma King, my mother's mother, lived in the Bronx, in a frame house a few blocks east of the Grand Concourse where my parents and I lived. It was dark outside when we walked across the street to her neighbor's apartment. There we were led into a warm, well-lighted room, with a round dining room table set with white plates and glowing with candles. "These are potato pancakes that Mrs. Simon has made for you and her boys," my grandma told us. The boys were bigger and older than Carol and I, and they wore corduroy knickers. Mrs. Simon filled our plates with pancakes, but first she and the boys sang a strange song in a strange language. Then we ate many pancakes, which Mrs. Simon called *latkes*.

After that *Chanukah* night, I remember sitting with my Grandma King, my mother, and her sisters in our kitchen, where we listened to the radio news of the Nazis invading Poland. Everyone was very worried about Jews being killed. I was six. And so it was in 1939, in the Bronx, that I became aware I was Jewish.

Many years would pass before I learned the truth of my family's heritage. My paternal grandparents, Samuel and Vera Schulmeister, were Jews from Ekaterinislav (now Dnipropetrovsk) in the Ukraine. Around the turn of the century, my grandfather was having trouble finding suitable jobs; his father-in-law, my great-grandfather Benjamin Ezachik—himself a practicing Jew— suggested that he convert to the Russian Orthodox faith. My grandfather then got a good job managing a department store in Omsk, Siberia. After a long journey across the steppes, the family—my grandparents, Aunt Frances, and her younger brother Arnold—settled in a house by the river Irtysh. My Aunt Frances told me many stories of this idyllic time, which came to an abrupt end when my grandmother became pregnant. Fearing that the baby would be a boy who would have to be circumcised and thus reveal them to be Jews, the family emigrated to America in 1905. My grandmother gave birth to a girl, who died the following year. My father was born in 1907.

Although Aunt Frances was greatly affected by her childhood experience as a Christian, my grandparents never truly gave up their Jewish identity, and Uncle Arnold and my father actually did not know about the conversion until they were much older. My grandmother spent her last years at the Hebrew Home for the Aged in Riverdale, in the Bronx, and she would warn my father, when he visited, not to speak to her in Russian because she remained ashamed of her Christian dalliance.

This started as a piece about celebrations—Christmas and *Chanukah*—and in a sense it is a celebration of discovery and of the power of memory and history in my life. ●

*Steve Johnson blessing Mark and Audrey on their first Shabbat
as Jews, camping in Waterford, Wisconsin, August 1979*

Shabbat Gifts

by Steve and Carol, Mark and Audrey Johnson

*W*e were preparing to become Jews, so Rabbi Arnold Rachlis suggested that we might make *Shabbat* special for our children by giving them small *Shabbat* gifts. Thereafter, every Friday, along with the candles, wine, and *challah,* our *Shabbat* table would hold two gifts: one for Mark and one for Audrey.

Over time this tradition served its purpose by making *Shabbat* special to two young children. In fact, it was our holy day of gifts.

In the final stages of our conversion process, we went to the *mikveh,* where we faced questions concerning our Jewish practices, our Jewish knowledge, and our Jewish intent. To include our whole family, the members of the *beit din* even asked questions of our seven-year-old son and our three-year-old daughter.

To Mark they asked, "Can you say the blessing for wine?" and he proudly proceeded to do so.

Then they asked Audrey, "What is your favorite holiday?" She did not answer. "Is your favorite holiday *Chanukah*?" She gave them a blank look. Then they explained, "*Chanukah* is the holiday when you receive presents." Audrey smiled brightly, clapped her hands, and cried, "Oh, yes. That is my favorite!"

It may have been *Chanukah* to them, but it was *Shabbat* to her. ●

An Alarming Purim

•••

by Elana Jacobs

I never miss any opportunity to dress up. The year I studied abroad at a *kibbutz* in Israel was no exception. That year's theme was queens–Queen Vashti, Queen Esther, Cleopatra, queen bee, drag queens–and creativity reigned.

I decided to dress up as a silver disco queen, beginning with a short, shimmery, sexy silver dress. In fact, I covered every inch of my body in silver, laced with tinsel as a substitute for a feather boa. I slathered my face with silver eye shadow and silver glitter, and painted my puckered lips with silver glitter. The final touch was my knee-high black leather boots. First, though, I had to adapt them to befit the legs of a silver disco queen. Tin foil did the trick, wrapped right up to my thigh. As a sexy disco queen, I happily marched in the *Purim* parade.

But I wasn't ready to retire my fabulous costume just yet. The following day I decided to maximize my *Purim* experience by taking the bus north to celebrate *Shushan Purim* in the walled city of Jerusalem. After all, how many times in my life would I be able to celebrate *Purim* for two whole days?

In Jerusalem my friends and I decided to attend the Great Synagogue to hear the *Megillah* reading. That year a special guest, Prime Minister Bibi Netanyahu, was in attendance. To deter the terrorist attacks that had marred previous *Purim* celebrations, ten metal detectors stood in the lobby. Amidst these high-security precautions there I stood, a silver disco queen with tin foil covering my legs. I waited in line patiently while all the security guards laughed. They made me go through the metal detector, and then they searched me individually with the security wand.

This search was humiliating, but it could have been worse. A little boy had brought in a toy gun, and all the security guards yelled at him. At least I didn't pose a security risk. Instead, my costume offered pure entertainment, lightening up the guards' long evening of security checks.

After twenty minutes, my friends and I left the Great Synagogue to go to another *shul.* Thankfully, this small building had attracted no one famous enough to require the installation of metal detectors. The moral of my story: to avoid holiday *tzuris,* make sure that when you decide to wear an aluminum foil *Purim* costume, you are the most famous person at your synagogue. ●

Zach (Haman) and Sarah (Esther) Lieberman, Purim 1982

The Whole Megillah

• •

by Syd Lieberman

When our kids were younger, they fit the stereotypes for girl and boy. Baby Sarah loved sitting in the middle of the living room, quietly stacking blocks. She radiated calm. We thought we were wonderful parents.

Then Zach came along to teach us humility. As a toddler, Zach would run into a room, hit a wall, bounce off with a grin, and keep going.

While Sarah made clothes for her Cabbage Patch doll, Zach carried around a box full of little plastic cars and trucks called Transformers. When twisted, turned, and tugged, these cars turned into robot monsters with names like Voltran, Megatron, Maladroid, Decepticon, and Autobot. One day when I complained that he was spending too much time with these toys, Zach whipped around in astonishment and confided, "Dad, you don't know it, but at this very moment, the Autobots are protecting the earth from the Decepticons."

At *Purim,* destined to be the beautiful Queen Esther, Sarah would drape herself in one of my wife Adrienne's old nightgowns. Then she'd add makeup, dangling earrings, and a veil.

A longer version of "The Whole Megillah" was published in
Streets and Alleys: Stories with a Chicago Accent (Little Rock,
Arkansas: August House, 1995).

Naturally, Zach would dress as the villainous Haman. This transformation required only an old bathrobe and a towel twisted to look like a turban. I would burn some cork and smudge a mustache and beard on his evil little Haman face.

I usually went to synagogue as a larger version of Haman, but Adrienne disdained Esther. A feminist, she preferred Vashti, the king's first wife who refused to dance for him and his cronies. She'd don an old robe, put her hair up in rollers, and carry a sign that read, "Not tonight, dear, I have a headache."

One night right before *Purim,* as we were finishing dinner, Adrienne said, "We always dress the same way. Why don't we try new costumes for *Purim* this year?"

"But I want to be Esther," Sarah whined.

"And I want to be Haman," I mimicked.

We all looked at Zach.

"I want dessert," he said.

Adrienne shrugged, realizing that this wasn't the right moment for innovation.

But the next night she repeated her plea for new *Purim* costumes. "Why don't we go as the *Megillah*?" she asked hopefully. I was baffled. The kids looked mystified, too. "You kids can go as the little *Megillah.* Dad and I will be the big *Megillah.*"

"It'll be great," Adrienne continued her sales pitch. "I'll print some of the story of Esther onto butcher paper. Then we'll roll the ends of the paper around us. So we'll be the poles. The story will spread between us. I know there's only one pole in the original–it just unwinds–but who will care?"

Sarah poked at her potatoes, unsure what this idea had to do with beauty. Zach suddenly decided to attack some peas.

Besides the fact that the *Megillah* scroll has only one post, Adrienne's idea had a serious flaw–binding Zachary and Sarah, a boy and a girl, a Haman and an Esther, into the same costume. They began to fight as soon as we rolled the paper on them.

"You're wearing the paper too high," shouted Zach.

"No, I'm not," said Sarah, dripping with more than her usual condescension. "You're wearing it too low."

"Mom, Sarah's got too much paper," Zach yelled.

"No, I don't," answered Sarah in the snooty tone older sisters hone to perfection. "You're the one that has too much."

"Let's hurry up and get them to the synagogue," Adrienne said to me. "Once the costume parade starts, they'll be fine."

I wasn't so sure, but I stowed our costume in the trunk and opened the back door of the car for the Sarah-and-Zach *Megillah* to slide in. Sarah gave me a look of exasperation. "You know, we're not going to be able to sit down," she complained.

"But I want to sit down," Zach whined.

"Just get in the car and stand in the back," Adrienne ordered. "We'll be there in a couple of minutes."

"I want to sit down," Zach repeated once he was in the car.

"Then sit," said his sister.

"But I can't if you don't."

"Well, I don't want to ruin the costume."

"Mom," shouted Zach.

"Mom," echoed Sarah.

They fought all the way to the synagogue, and they fought all the way through the reading of the *Megillah.* They weren't even happy when they got to spin their noisy *greggers* at the sound of Haman's name.

Still, I had actually begun to like the new costumes. They were easily the most creative in the sanctuary, and when we had entered, we had received approving laughter. But Adrienne seemed to be growing more depressed by the minute.

"It's going to be all right," I reassured her. "They'll be fine when everyone starts to admire their costume."

We lined up to march around the synagogue. The kids were right in front of us, glowering at each other. In front of them stood the *matzo*-ball family, father and sons stuffed into yellow costumes designed to look like *matzo* balls. The mother followed in a baseball uniform, swinging a baseball bat. Behind us a woman marched in green tights, green sweater, green hat, and a colorful collar. "Who are you?" I asked.

"Why, Queen Aster," she replied.

As soon as we started marching, the battle raged anew.

"You're walking too fast," Sarah complained. "Slow down."

Zach didn't bother to answer. He had just realized that his big sister was attached to him just as much as he was attached to her. He began to speed up.

"Dad," yelled Sarah over her shoulder, looking like a passenger on a runaway train. But there was nothing I could do. Zach was the engine.

"Go left," Sarah shouted, as they came to the end of the aisle. After all, that's where the parade was headed. But Zach turned right, striking out on his own.

This was too much for Sarah. "Zachary, stop this instant," she screamed. Then she stopped. Zach jerked back like a fish on a hook. For a second he stopped and stared at Sarah angrily. Then an idea occurred to him. He smiled at her and at us, then turned and ran at full speed. Sarah dug in her heels and the paper ripped in two.

Zach happily ran up and down the aisles, his portion of the *Megillah* trailing like a banner. We consoled a crestfallen Sarah with some *hamantaschen,* and she soon ran off to play with her friends.

Later Zach charged up to us. "Great costume, Mom," he announced. "Let's do it again next year." Then he was off, flying around the outside of the synagogue, his friends chasing after him, as if he were rallying them in the Decepticons' eternal battle against the Autobots. ●

Cross-Dressing, Jewish Style

by Fran Landt

When I was young, picking a costume for *Purim* offered one more demonstration of gender inequality. While a boy could dress as Mordecai, Ahashverosh, or Haman, most girls were afraid to dress as anybody but Esther. And Esther had to be the stereotype of femininity.

One *Purim,* my mother helped me create a Middle-Eastern styled Esther costume, using a striped silk robe and scarves. I returned from Sunday school disgusted because the prize for the best Esther had gone to a girl in a frilly and fluffy pink party dress. My sister Jan, however, refused to dress as Esther. Since no girl had yet dared to dress as Vashti, Jan came up with a novel solution. She went as Mordecai and stole the show. ●

*Joel Gratch and Jordan Margolis in a scene
from the JRC Purim Spiel,* Bali Chai, *March 2000*

Milking Purim for What It's Worth

by Ellen Rosen Kaplan

*I*t was the year 5757/1997. It was *Purim.* My husband, four-year-old daughter, four-month-old son, and I traveled to Southfield, Michigan, for the *Bat Mitzvah* of a dear friend's daughter. We arrived at the synagogue at 9:30 A.M. dressed in our *Purim* costumes, but no one was around. Since we had remembered to turn our watches ahead one hour to account for the time difference, we double-checked the invitation to make sure that we were in fact on time. Perplexed by the absence of the usual *Purim* fanfare, we rechecked our invitation to make sure the address and name of the synagogue matched the words and numbers on the building we had entered. They did. Clearly something was wrong, but we had no idea what. Could they have changed the time and simply forgotten to contact us since we were coming from out-of-town? In our black-and-white cow costumes, we waited.

Finally we saw a woman who looked a bit confused herself. "Are you here for Dayna's *Bat Mitzvah*?" I asked.

She looked at me and laughed, "Yes, are you?"

"Yes. But where's your costume?" I wondered.

"Oh, I didn't wear one. I guess I just couldn't get it together."

"Oh," I said as I scanned my herd, "I certainly hope you are in the minority."

Ellen Rosen Kaplan, her husband Leonard, and their children, Jordan and Hannah, Purim 1997

So we waited together to see who else would show up.

Eventually, I heard what sounded like muffled song and prayer and motioned for my family to follow me. We opened a heavy door to find a sanctuary filled with people in ordinary *Shabbat* clothes. Nobody was wearing a costume. All eyes turned toward us. Several official-looking men approached us and politely explained that the *Purim* service would take place the next day. Since the *Bat Mitzvah* had specifically been scheduled to coincide with *Purim*—which happened to fall on a Sunday this year—the *Bat Mitzvah* would not be part of the *Shabbat* morning service, as it usually is.

With our tails between our legs, we sheepishly mooed our way out of the Conservative sanctuary. The rabbi did not seem to find any humor in the sight of three upright cows, plus one calf snuggling in his Baby Bjorn. We were soon beside ourselves with hysterics. Laughing with us, the noncostumed woman who had also come a day early, took out her cell phone and called my friend Roni to report our misadventure.

By the time we arrived at 9:30 the next morning, everyone at the *Bat Mitzvah* already knew who we were: the four cows who had shown up one day too soon. Well, that certainly was one way to meet people quickly. So we milked it for all it was worth. ●

Gioret Purim

by Marie Davidson

As a *gioret*–convert to Judaism–I had a lot to learn about being Jewish. Luckily, I received a special kind of total Jewish immersion when, a scant sixteen months after my trip to the *mikveh,* my husband and I went off to Israel for a ten-month stay.

Of all my *gioret* holidays, *Purim* stands out. For one thing, it snowed that year, 1980. For several months, Larry and I had been freezing in an apartment that lacked central heat between 9 A.M. and 3 P.M. With a record-breaking rainy season seeping into our bones, we somehow felt prepared for the snow. But snow in Jerusalem is a rare event, and it threw our Jerusalemite friends for a loop. "Jerusalem is cut off!" the radio announcer cried. From Tel Aviv, trainloads of amazed Israelis came to witness the spectacle. We were greatly amused.

That year we went to not one, but three, *Purim* parties. Some American friends hosted the first, and they asked guests to come dressed as their favorite religious figures. Feeling frivolously paganish, I went as the Egyptian goddess Isis. My costume involved a newly-bought *galabiyah,* some aluminum foil "jewelry," and plenty of eye makeup.

Larry went as the Pope. He wore a sheet; a cardboard mitre decorated with magic marker; and, as his stola, a scarf sporting sayings like *pax vobiscum, carpe diem,* and *caveat emptor.* This costume made a big hit, partly because it gave other guests an unprecedented chance to say, "Good *Yontiff,* Pontiff." He even sort of looked like the Pope.

Later that evening, we attended a party in our apartment building. There we learned how limited our *ulpan* Hebrew was when we listened to young Israelis talking fast with a lot of slang. We were humbled to find ourselves falling back on safe phrases like *eyfoh ha-yayeen?* ("Where's the wine?")

Our third party took place at the *yeshivah* where we studied part-time, in the Baka neighborhood of Jerusalem. In our Isis and Pope costumes we trekked through the snow to the *yeshivah.* Laughing soldiers on half-tracks glided by, searching for people to "save" from nonexistent snowdrifts.

At the *yeshivah* one of the Pardes faculty, costumed unimaginatively in his army uniform, chanted the *Megillah* of Esther. Men and women listeners stood on either side of a more-or-less symbolic *mechitzah.* We all booed at the name of Haman. At each mention of Esther's name, we women sent up a cascade of soprano "yays!" One of the other students–an American from New Jersey–had come dressed as a Prohibition-era gangster. After the *Megillah* reading, this self-styled gangster strode up to Larry, cocked his plastic machine-gun, and ordered, "Lay *tefillin,* Holy Father!" And this is how I came to have a photo of the Pope wearing phylacteries.

The following day was *Shushan Purim,* a continuation of the holiday celebrated only in walled cities dating from the original *Purim.* Larry and I walked around Jerusalem, photographing the snow-covered buildings and walls. Most people had gone back to work activities. But Orthodox men in their black hats and long beards continued their celebration.

Some had obviously been drinking. One, a young *Hasidic*

man, greeted us heartily and winked at me. In a sober state, he would undoubtedly have said nothing and probably also averted his eyes to avoid a direct gaze. A former Catholic, I understood this tactic: the avoidance of occasions of "sin." But on *Purim,* everything is supposed to be upside down and backwards. This young man had obviously followed the holiday prescription to imbibe *ad lo yada,* until you didn't know the difference between "blessed be Mordecai" and "cursed be Haman." As he relaxed his usual inhibitions during this annual festival of letting it hang out, we shared a laugh.

Two days later, the snow had completely melted, and *Pesach* lay around the corner. Our neighbors began their annual frenzy of spring cleaning. I had no wish to join in this exhausting enterprise, but I continued to delight in the Jewish year unfolding in Jerusalem, the most Jewish of places. ●

Havdalah Essentials

by Naomi Feldman

*T*here we were in Israel, Dan and I, I for the first time and, of course, overwhelmed by the myriad sights, smells, tastes, sounds. It was unbelievably cold, not only in Safed where we were to spend *Shabbat,* but throughout the country. On our arrival in Safed, we left Dan's son, Larry, so that he could go about the Orthodox rituals he needed to follow in order to greet the Sabbath, while we spent the night with an electric radiator pulled close to our bed. The following day, after putting on as many warm layers as possible, we walked the streets, visiting art studios, and trying to satisfy our curiosity about the synagogues we passed. We peered in when we could and listened to the sounds of *davening* from the sidewalk when we could not.

At sundown, Larry joined us for *Havdalah.* We knew that we needed three things—a spice box, wine, and a braided candle—and we also knew that we had none of them. Larry, however, was not only a bright kid but a smart *yeshivah* student as well. To meet the first requirement, the spice box, Larry borrowed Dan's traveling tobacco pouch. To substitute for the wine, he went to the hotel lobby and returned with a can of Coke. We did in fact have a candle in our hotel room (as most hotel rooms in Israel do, in case of a power failure). Using Dan's pocket knife, Larry cut

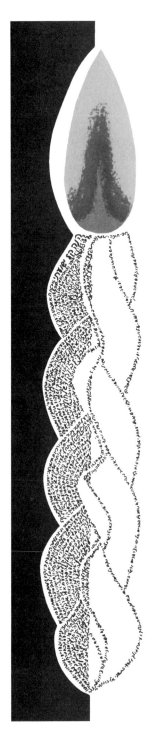

the candle in half, removed enough wax from the "new" candle to make a usable wick, then lit them and held them together to braid their flames.

And so we celebrated *Havdalah* just as we should have. This remains a special memory for all of us. Larry's creative combination of practicality and theology seems to me an example of what has enabled Judaism to survive.

We love the fact that a few years later, when Dan and I married, Larry's wedding gift to us was a framed print by a Safed artist—a stylized *Havdalah* candle whose braid is made of calligraphy. What could be more appropriate? ●

"Havdalah" by Safed artist, Nechama

Tuesday Night Dinners

by Laurie Kahn

*T*he *Torah* includes no direct references to Tuesday night dinners. The Talmudic masters seemed to have been unaware of it. This sacred ritual emerged at a time in which the meanings sustaining my life shattered. A time in which our family rituals became like trying to squeeze into a too-small pair of pants. After checking to see if the seams could be let out, I realized that I had to surrender and start over.

My marriage ended. The racy details about the twenty-year-old secretary are probably not relevant. I became a single parent with the task of recreating a family. My daughter, Emily, was nine years old; my stepson, Matthew, was twelve; and, just to keep life interesting, my best friend's eighteen-year-old daughter, Madeleine, had moved into our basement as a kind of halfway house to independence. Why and how we all belonged together was not obvious to the untrained eye. What was clear was that these children needed me and I needed them.

I would like to say that after much consideration and study of the best aspects of Sabbath, Passover, and Super Bowl Sunday, I came up with an idea for something that would sustain our spirits. But this was not the case. I was working hard to increase my income in order to keep the house my children called home.

So I asked the children to take responsibility for Tuesday night dinners. I would supply the money for groceries, and the rest would be up to them. I imposed no culinary expectations; the only requirement was that they do it together. The first few Tuesdays had a macaroni-and-cheese theme. One dinner had three different varieties of macaroni and cheese, with a side of grilled cheese sandwiches and potato chips. My job was to express gratitude and take pleasure in their collective efforts.

We soon added another rule to Tuesday night dinners; anyone was welcome as long as he or she participated in some aspect of the meal. My children began to bring their friends. Stray kids from the neighborhood could be found chopping vegetables for salad, mopping the floor, or running to the grocery store for a forgotten ingredient.

Matthew's best friend, Jake, was a regular, sometimes dragging along his six-year-old brother, Joey. Joey took charge of putting napkins on the table. Ricardo, the kid with the glass eye who was struggling to stay in high school, became another occasional visitor. On his first visit, Ricardo plopped himself down, ready to eat. A free meal: what could be bad? Afterwards, he rose to leave. "Hey, Ricardo, you're on dishes tonight," someone advised. Ricardo was stunned. Under his breath he whispered, "I've never done dishes." I assured him I would teach him everything he needed to know. He smiled and rolled up his sleeves.

Later that spring, Ricardo again showed up on a Tuesday night for our ritual dinner. After setting the table, he sat down with his report card in hand. He passed it around, right after the mashed potatoes. It was all C's and D's, which meant he would graduate. We all cheered.

Topics of friendship, justice, disappointments, dreams, and triumphs make up the steady banter of these dinners, and laughter is a constant companion. Though we light no candles and say no blessing over the bread, and the preferred drink is Pepsi and not wine, we do take turns saying a blessing before we eat. One night Emily's friend Nina volunteered. As we bowed our heads, she prayed, "Please, God, bless my new rock-and-roll band and help us to make a CD. Amen."

Over the years the food has improved, moving from macaroni and fish sticks to full-course meals. Some of the regulars have moved on to college. The younger children have now become the head chefs.

Yet on Tuesday nights, there is no doubt where we belong and what matters. All other activities stand in line behind our gathering. Classes, after-school activities, work emergencies—even my son's football practice—could never interfere. None of us would allow it. For here we have discovered that even the ordinary can become sacred. Everyone whose life has been touched by this blessed event knows that on Tuesday nights, there is a meal waiting and everyone is welcome. ●

Our Passover Odyssey

....

by Bobbie Berkowitz

*B*arry came from a traditional background, while *kosher* was a foreign word in my family. When I was young, I enjoyed the *Sedarim* my grandfather led. At these family *Sedarim,* we listened to music sung on old phonograph records.

Because of the different ways our families celebrated *Pesach,* Barry and I have been evolving in our own observance for as long as we have been married. In fact, almost three months after our wedding in 1965, *Pesach* triggered our first argument. I offered to set aside our unused "good" dishes to use for *Pesach.* That wasn't necessary, Barry said. But he insisted that we buy special Passover food.

"It costs too much," I complained, "especially the meat." And I was sure kosher meat wouldn't be as tasty as supermarket meat. Eventually Barry and tradition won, and, from then on, all our *Pesach* food was "Kosher for Passover."

Our daughters remember the Passover boxes their dad sent them at college. When they admitted they didn't eat the food, I asked Barry why he continued mailing the packages. His response was that it was his job to send the food and the girls' job to eat it. So, he would continue doing his job even if they didn't do theirs.

Thirty years after we married, one of our daughters became engaged. Since her fiancé was religiously observant, we decided to do more than just have special kosher food for Passover. I went shopping for new pots, pans, plates, and utensils. I even bought separate dish drainers for milk and meat dishes. At the end of the holiday, we packed up everything and stored it in the basement.

I could hardly believe what we had done. I used to listen in amazement as friends would tell how their parents pulled out their Passover things for one week every year. Now we were doing the same thing.

When we moved to a new home where we keep kosher all year round, we began to do even more to observe *Pesach*. First we took all our metal and glass kitchen items to the *mikveh*. Then the pantries got a thorough cleaning. Regular food went into sealed cabinets. We arranged for a rabbi to sell our *chametz* for the Passover period. And, in order to do some cooking ahead of the holiday, we even installed a *Pesach* stove in the basement. This amused the man who put in the extra stove, because he knew how little we used our regular one.

Over the years—almost as many years as the Jews wandered in the desert—we have made *Pesach* into a major observance. One of our sons-in-law has introduced us to Sephardic delicacies, while the other has led us in meaningful *Sedarim.* Now we look forward to our grandchildren reading the Four Questions, searching for the *afikomen,* and continuing these Jewish traditions. ●

Clara and Morriss Powitz, parents of Charlene Gelber, c. 1975

The Leftover Memory

by Charlene Gelber

*I*t was the last Passover my mother, Clara, was able to celebrate with our family. She had Alzheimer's disease, and two months later I would return to place her in a nursing home. But, for now, I was visiting my parents to make *Seder* in their Florida condo.

My father had specifically requested the fried *matzo*-meal pancakes he loved so much and had not had in a long time. Following his suggestion, I seated my mother in the kitchen and gave her a bowl with some *matzo*-meal mixture so she could feel part of the cooking process. I stood at the stove, ankles swelling and back hurting, frying batches and batches of pancakes until I filled their largest casserole dish. I cooked more food, cleaned the kitchen several times, set the table, and finally sat down, exhausted, as my father began the *Seder*.

"Let's eat!" was the unanimous cry when the last cup of wine was drained. My husband took the huge serving dish of *matzo*-meal pancakes from the counter to bring to the table, when the gigantic bowl fell from his hands, hit the floor with a loud crash, and shattered throughout the room. Pancakes mingled everywhere with glass across the recently cleaned kitchen floor. I screamed and ran, skidding on oily, mushy debris, until I reached the door and escaped to the catwalk. Leaning over the railing, I exploded into sobs that were about more than lost pancakes.

"Look at this," my husband said as he came out the door to check on me, a sheepish grin on his face. Securely in his hands was a box of oatmeal.

"Read the label on top of the cover," he said, handing me the box. Printed in my father's hand was the word "capshuts."

"So, what do you think is in here?" my husband smugly asked.

I thought for a second or two and stated, with my best know-it-all voice, "Those plastic round tops that you put on soda bottles to seal them when you've removed the original cap."

"OK," he said, "open up the box."

I opened the box, which was filled to the brim with individual restaurant packages of ketchup. Now we were both laughing. My husband had redeemed himself, and we went in to clean up the pancakes and eat.

When my mother died several years later, my father gave me her wedding rings. Those rings, which had been kept safe on her finger and removed only when she was admitted to the nursing home, were her most valued possession, her only real jewelry. It took several years for me to decide to wear them. Then I took the rings to a jeweler to be sized and cleaned.

Looking at the rings through his loupe, the jeweler asked, "What's the hard material embedded underneath the stones?"

"Let me look," I replied.

But I didn't need the magnifying eyepiece. One look started me giggling. All these many years later, hardened into a fossil, lay the evidence of our last *Seder* together. The Passover pancakes may never have made it to the *Seder* table, but the mixture had stayed preserved in my mother's rings. *Dayenu!* ●

A Passover Progression

Or: If I can see the Seder plate from where I'm sitting, am I finally a grown up?

••

by Lynn Pollack

*I*n my family of origin, religious observance was almost completely taboo. Nevertheless, we did attend Passover *Sedarim* at my Uncle Jack and Aunt Riv's; she was my mother's only sibling. We went for only one night, the second one, because my mother claimed that it was always nicer. Everyone's more relaxed, less anxious, she said. Hungry for any morsel of religion from my devoutly atheist mother, I accepted this declaration unquestioningly.

Riv and Jack's *Sedarim* were conducted in their living room, with thirty to forty guests positioned along a bowling alley stretch of tables, arranged highest to lowest. Uncle Jack, the *Seder* leader, posted himself at the tall end, subtly looking down on those at the far end.

And that, of course, is where my two brothers and I were always seated. From this distance, I could barely hear my uncle as he droned on with tidbits of wisdom from this or that rabbi. I always assumed that if I could hear what he was saying, I would find it interesting. My brother Richard assumed the opposite. And my brother David tried to figure out how to transform his wine glass into a bottomless cup, bypassing the grape juice completely. By the end of the *Seder,* David was always as red as the horseradish, and my aunt, who loved him dearly, would cup his cheeks and say, "Davila, is it too hot in here for you, darling?"

During the *Seder* our chief entertainment was trying to flip *matzo* balls from one soup bowl into another. Since we never could get to the middle of one of Riv's golf-ball *k'neidlach*—and we didn't dare pop one in our mouths—we believed there really were rubber bands at their core, which explained why they bounced so well.

Flash forward. I am twenty-four, out of college, working, living on my own. I quietly announce to my parents that I am driving to Minneapolis with the Jewish man I've just started dating, to spend Passover with his family. Their reaction surprises me. Instead of *kvelling,* they quiver. I am confused. After all, they had not seemed particularly thrilled with my previous four boyfriends, who had numbered three Catholics and a Communist. My mother had gone berserk when my brother David married a Unitarian. What exactly did she have in mind for me? Years later, I realized that the prospect of a traditional, observant son-in-law was a little too much for my mother. For her my perfect mate would have been a secular Jew, the kind of guy whose Hebrew is limited to a hearty *"L'chaim!"* at appropriate moments.

So, Mike and I drove up to Minneapolis. I would finally experience a first *Seder.* Once there, I again found myself seated at the bottom of the table, surrounded by the four Okrent brothers. The two sisters mostly bobbed and served. Though only about twelve of us sat around that table, it seemed like forty to me.

At the head of the table, Mike's father conducted the service, largely in Hebrew. I can still hear Sam intoning "I and not a messenger." Perhaps those words stick with me because they were the only English. Meanwhile, down at my end of the table, the brothers were flinging popovers at each other and retelling

Lynn Pollack and Mike Okrent, September 4, 1977

stories and myths that were totally irrelevant to Passover but apparently traditional to every family gathering. They were so loud that I kept expecting Mike's father to erupt. But he droned on, oblivious to all. Later on, Mike's sisters came out of the kitchen long enough to join us for a raucous rendition of the *Birkat ha-Mazon.* Having never witnessed such fervor and enjoyment, coupled with complete disrespect and irreverence, I truly thought I had stumbled upon a little-known branch of Judaism.

Before another Passover came and went, Mike and I got married. And as long as Sam lived, he continued to lead the *Sedarim* at one end, while the boys at the other end slung popovers and stories at each other. But then Sam was gone, and a whole new generation sat at the far end of the table. The brothers took turns leading the *Sedarim.* It seemed strange at first, but eventually we grew into the new arrangement. Now, nearly twenty years after Sam's death, I tend to sit pretty close to the leader, with a great view of the *Seder* plate. I'm sure I could even lead a *Seder* myself. And I do think my mother was right: the second *Seder* is always nicer than the first. Only now, I understand that it helps to have had that first *Seder,* too. ●

Carol Brumer (left) and her family on Passover c. 1973

A Kosher Kodak Moment

• •

by Carol Brumer

I grew up in the shadow of Notre Dame University, in the St. Joe Valley (population 300,000), where there were 250 Jewish families. In the 1970s, Jewish life in St. Joe was barely visible outside the Jewish community. The one exception I clearly remember was the annual family photo around a *Seder* table, which appeared in the *South Bend Tribune* a few days before Passover. I naively presumed that the families were chosen by the local synagogues, or were plucked from obscurity like a would-be actress discovered at a drugstore, or otherwise merited some special recognition.

When I was fifteen, I noticed less than three days before the *Seder* that the photo had not yet appeared. I mused out loud about it to my mother as I went off to school and immediately forgot my comment.

The next day I came home from school at 3 P.M. and the *Seder* table had been set with the special glassware, china, and silver—still a day away from the actual event. My mother urged me, my siblings (Barry, age twelve, and Susie, age four), and my father, a teacher, to hurry and get dressed in *Shabbos* clothes, because photographers were coming to take our family picture for the paper.

I couldn't believe it! It seemed like magic. I remembered my comment, and suddenly here we were. The photo appeared the very next day in the paper, as Jewish families all over America, and especially in South Bend, gathered around their *Seder* tables.

As I grew a bit older, I realized that the Passover miracle in our house that year had not been Elijah coming to visit. Instead, my mother's quick thinking and her call to the paper allowed our family to be featured that year—a Reconstructionist-style miracle. ●

I'll Always Remember Uncle Max

by Roslyn Goodman Levinson

When I was fourteen, my widowed mother remarried and
we moved from Chicago, where we had been living for a year,
back to Dubuque where I had spent my first twelve years. My
stepfather had a large family, all of whom lived in various Iowa
towns within one hundred miles of Dubuque. I had been told
that on Passover family members pack their cars with fragrant
traditional specialties, freshly prepared, and drive to Aunt Esther's
Dubuque home for the annual celebration.

Apprehensive about the first Passover with my new family,
I wonder, "Will they like me? Will they accept me?"

A genial woman with large, smiling brown eyes and abundant
energy, Aunt Esther greets me, "Welcome, welcome." She wears
a cumbersome bib apron to protect her good dress as she
balances contributions from guests in her strong, work-hardened
arms: fragrant carrot *tzimmes,* brown-crusted potato *kugel,* bottles
of wine, leafy green vegetable salads, and my favorite, *charoses*
(nuts, dates, and apples chopped together and bound with sweet
red wine).

There is little space and fewer chairs in the living room
because tables stretch from the farthest end of this room through

A longer version, "My Unforgettable Seder With Uncle Max,"
was published in the *Evanston Review*, March 28, 2002.

the dining room to the kitchen door. The layout of her house reminds me of the shot-gun houses I had seen in New Orleans where each room opened into the other in a straight line, and a bullet shot through the front door would whistle straight through and out the back door.

No matter where you are in her house, the pleasure of pungent odors emanating from the kitchen is somewhat overpowered by the smell of the *gefilte fish* that Aunt Esther had made from scratch. "None of that canned stuff in my house!" she proclaims. "I buy my fish fresh, scale it, chop it and cook it myself." Those who grew up on Aunt Esther's *gefilte fish* agree, "Hers is the best."

More than twenty family members gather here: Uncle Max, Uncle Charlie, Aunt Gitel, Aunt Ida, Aunt Eva, Louis, my stepfather, their spouses and all ages of children and grandchildren. I think that becoming a part of such a large family will take some getting used to for me. My father died when I was seven, so since then our Passover *Sedarim* had included only my mother, my grandmother (who lived with us until Mother remarried), and me. But I soon warm to their hospitality and their kidding.

At sunset, Uncle Louie, Aunt Esther's husband, encourages us to sit down at the table so he can begin the *Seder.* Uncle Louie, a small, gentle man whose warm blue eyes smile shyly at the children, sits at the head of the table in the living room. Aunt Esther sits at the end of the table near the kitchen door. The others disperse to find seats around the table. Genial Uncle Max, the eldest, a big man with a fringe of white hair neatly trimmed around his bald head, takes a chair in the middle under the arch that separates the two front rooms.

When we are all seated, Uncle Louie says, "Esther, please light the candles." Two candles in tall ornate silver candlesticks had been placed on the table in front of Aunt Esther. Covering her head with a lace handkerchief, Aunt Esther strikes a wooden match against the rough strip of sand paper on the match box, lights the candles, and says the prayer to usher in the holiday. Our host then pours the first glass of wine for each adult and grape juice for the children. "How soon can I drink it?" I whisper to my mother. "Not yet," she replies. Uncle Louie chants the *Kiddush,* the prayer over the wine, and drinks a glassful. Each of us has a paperback *Haggadah* that contains readings, prayers, and songs—the rituals of the entire service, the entire Passover story of the Jews' Exodus from Egypt.

Having only eaten a few bites of *matzo* combined with *charoses* and bitter herbs from the *Seder* plate, I am ravenous by the time Aunt Esther brings us each a bowl of steaming soup. It doesn't take long for everyone, including us children, to devour the rich chicken broth and fluffy delicate *matzo* balls. Oval balls of *gefilte fish,* each studded with an orange slice of cooked carrot, follow the soup. "Max, please pass the horseradish around," Aunt Esther says. The beet-red horseradish meant to accompany the fish happens to be in the middle of the long table and in front of Uncle Max, who graciously grants Aunt Esther's request.

After the *gefilte fish* is eaten and those plates removed to the kitchen, Aunt Esther and her sister and sisters-in-law bring in large platters of fragrant baked chicken, potato *kugel,* vegetables, salad, beef brisket, and the carrot and sweet potato *tzimmes,* placing them in a row down the table so they can be passed. I have never seen a table laden with so much food. Eagerly we begin passing the dishes around the table. I heap my plate and can barely wait to start eating.

"Max, will you pass the chicken?" Aunt Gitel asks.

"Coming right up," says Max, a warm grin filling his face as he puts his fork down and lifts the large platter with both hands to pass it down the table to his sister.

A few minutes later one of the children asks, "May I have potato *kugel?*"

"Sure you can," says Max as he reaches to his right and sends the *kugel* down to the other end of the table.

Poor Max, sitting in the middle of the table closest to the platters and bowls, is so busy passing food that he hardly has time to lift his fork to his mouth. As we become aware of his dilemma, it becomes a joke and the children begin asking Uncle Max to pass various foods to them.

"That's all I'm going to pass until everyone finishes what's on his plate," Max announces, "and that includes what is on my plate!" He looks around the table at the smiling faces, realizes he is the victim of a joke, and begins to laugh. We all join in. From that day forward, whoever is asked to pass the food at dinner, we call an "Uncle Max."

Although many years have passed since that *Seder,* I will always remember it for the warmth I felt being among my new family and for its fulfillment of the wonderful Passover traditions. And I will always remember Uncle Max. ●

Worth the Wait

• •

by Emily J. Harris

*M*y father had an incredible sense of direction and was
compulsively prompt, except on Passover. No matter what time
we left Manhattan for Cousins Fred and Edna's house, it was
always rush hour. When we finally made it to Connecticut, we'd
be lost in a mass of indistinguishable street names—Grove Lane,
Grove Avenue, Grove Place, Grove Road—all of which seemed to
end in cul de sacs. Asking for directions was out of the question.
Instead, my father wondered each year why Connecticut couldn't
use a grid system. When we finally arrived, my new spring
clothes were crumpled after hours in the back seat, and the
macaroons from our local bakery were gone.

Fred and Edna were our only Orthodox relatives and the only
observant members of our family. Each year we read the entire
Haggadah in both Hebrew and English. And each year their son,
Harold, grew more religious. As a teenager he grew *payis,* and
decided that the *matzo* the rest of us ate wasn't kosher enough
for him; he imported his own from Israel. I felt embarrassed as
he sat apart from the table, swaying and chanting. I was alarmed
when he turned beet red as he ate an entire circular *matzo* that
was completely covered with freshly ground *maror.*

Although I remained mystified by Harold, as I got older, I grew less impatient with the *Seder*. When I was in high school, Fred—who seemed to become more liberal as his son grew more intensely observant—initiated a discussion about how much Hebrew to use in the *Seder*. I surprised myself by saying that even though I didn't know a word of Hebrew, we should keep both languages to help us stay connected to Jews all over the world who were saying the same words at the same time. And even though the *Seder* was quite lengthy, it always seemed worth the wait for dinner. ●

Passover Giggles

by Cheryl Bondy Kaplan

*U*ntil I was an adult, I never knew that a *Seder* was supposed to be a serious religious ritual. Our family *Sedarim* were of the hysterical variety, and to this day the mere thought of a *Seder* makes me giggle.

Though not related by blood, the Rosenfeld and Bondy clans were close enough to be quasi-relatives. Too close to call the adults Mr. and Mrs., we settled on Uncle and Aunt, and the three girls from each family acted like cousins. The two families have always spent Passover *Sedarim* and *Yom Kippur* break-fasts together. The Rosenfelds hosted Passover, and we hosted the break-fast, with the cooking shared by the mothers of both families.

We arrived at the Rosenfelds in the late afternoon before the first *Seder.* While our mothers put together the last-minute details of the feast, we explored our "cousins'" latest jewelry, clothing, toy, or cat acquisitions. In the living room, the Rosenfelds' feuding *Bubbes* sat silently, as far away from each other as possible, clearly not pleased to be in each other's company. (I never did find out why they didn't get along.) Moving on to the *Seder,* the grown-ups settled us at the table, separating us as best they could.

Immediately, we would start to giggle, without even a joke or

Family of Cheryl Bondy Kaplan, Passover 1991

quip—pure, unadulterated laughter brought on merely by sitting down at the *Seder* table. The first snickers were easy to squelch, but as we began taking turns reading, the laughter became uncontrollable—not just quiet chuckling, but pee-in-your-pants, Jello-through-the-nostrils howling that was completely contagious to anyone under the age of fifteen. I'm not sure if the gaiety was induced by our anticipation of the sweet *Mogen David* or by the prohibition against silly behavior. Either way, by the time we were old enough to partake in the annual four cups, we were completely insane at the *Seder* table.

Sure, our parents doled out the obligatory admonishments to get serious, but they knew their efforts were futile. So they just winked at each other, tried to maintain some level of order, and forged ahead through the Maxwell House® *Haggadah.* In retrospect, I think they probably enjoyed watching their children, all together at the festive holiday, experiencing pure joy—a tad inappropriate for the occasion, but joy nevertheless. ●

Legacy

by Mel Patrell Furman

I never made Passover with my mother-in-law. Although I knew
her for seven years and attended her *Sedarim* while dating her
son, I was never asked to be involved in the preparations. Yet her
memory is a palpable presence in my kitchen every spring as I
clean and cook for Passover.

My husband's family was not particularly religious, but they
observed Passover meticulously when his mother was alive. My
mother-in-law would clean the entire house, then she would
empty and clean each kitchen cabinet and drawer, and move all
food to a storage closet outside the kitchen for the duration of
Passover. She would lock away all the everyday dishes and pots
and pans in cabinets that she would tape shut and mark "not for
Passover" to avoid the possibility that someone might inadvertently
take out and use these items. She had another full set of cooking
paraphernalia and dishes used only that one week of the
year. Brought up an assimilated Italian, she had assumed the
Eastern European traditions of her husband's family and carried the
burden of them gracefully.

The first time I came to the *Seder,* as her son's non-Jewish
girlfriend, the evening began with her apology. "I'm sorry all the
food tastes so bad," she said with a thick Italian accent. "It's

Passover. We can't have normal food. To be a Jew means to suffer. That's why we have Passover. To remind us."

I was astonished. But then we sat down. My boyfriend, Boris, was leading the *Seder,* a lengthy service performed entirely at the dinner table. Although I didn't understand the Hebrew at all, I could follow along in English through the much-maligned Maxwell House® *Haggadah,* ubiquitous because General Foods gave them away by the tens of thousands as a supermarket promotion. I was quickly captivated by the service and its symbols. The Four Questions, asked that year by Boris's fourteen-year-old sister, emphasize the *Seder's* educational purpose. Ancient words call all who are hungry to come and eat from the bread of affliction. Jews remember the bitter tears of their enslavement in Egypt even as they welcome spring, with the ritual eating of a sprig of parsley dipped in salt water. *Matzo,* the bread of slaves, recalls the haste of their departure, when they literally had no time to let the dough rise before baking.

That *Seder* I sat with people who had jumped out of the mouth of Hitler. For many at the table, the Passover account of running away in haste from all the familiars of life was more than ancient history; it echoed their own childhoods in Europe. As a young American woman who had never before met a Holocaust survivor, I sat among victims of the worst sort of enslavement and celebrated with them the value of history and of freedom. Although an outsider, I felt welcome and included. It was a monumental experience.

It didn't all go smoothly. At one point during the *Seder,* my future mother-in-law came to the table with a basin and a pitcher of water. She leaned over the table and offered the basin to Boris's brother, Phil, who was sitting a few seats away from me. He put his hands over the basin, and she poured water over them in a ritual hand washing. She moved on to the next person at the table, Boris's father. Then she washed Boris's hands. Next in line, I put up my hands for my turn. She frowned and shook her head. "No." I put my hands back in my lap, red-faced. Their custom was to wash the hands of the men only.

Boris was in his element as the leader, fluent in Hebrew and well-versed in the *Haggadah* text. He had been leading the *Seder* since age eleven, when he inherited the role from his grandfather. Boris often asked questions to invite participation and discussion, and he gloried in fielding the inevitable follow-up questions. His siblings grumbled about the wait for dinner, which was served at a fixed point in the narration and thus delayed by every digression. Up and down the table an undercurrent of whispers—"Hurry up, hurry up,"—grew less subtle as the evening progressed. Boris paid no attention.

Another surprise came during the festive meal. Never a big fan of Jewish food, I declined the *gefilte fish* and sampled the *matzo*-ball soup without enthusiasm. But then I tasted for the first time something unique and unforgettable, a stew of brisket with onions, sweet potatoes, and prunes in a sauce laced with honey—in Yiddish, a *tzimmes.* I still think of this dish as a gift from my mother-in-law.

The gifts were few. Three years later, when Boris announced his intention to marry me, his parents were adamantly opposed. Long welcomed as a guest in their home, I was suddenly banished. We put our wedding plans on hold. That year the *Seder* came and went without my even looking up from my box of tissues. But the following year my officemate invited me to a *Seder* at her boyfriend's house, and I arrived enthusiastically, carrying a brisket *tzimmes.* The next year my roommate and I hosted a *Seder* for twenty-four in our Cambridge apartment with borrowed tables and chairs.

A few months later Boris and I married. We moved to Chicago

Jonah Furman, Passover 1991

and my free-form Cambridge *Seder* was no more. That next spring there was no *Seder*. My mother-in-law was dying, and I ate salad off paper plates in our Chicago apartment while Boris sat at her bedside in a Boston hospital.

The following year the burden of the *Seder* fell on me. By then we had moved from Boris's bachelor pad to a three-bedroom vintage apartment, complete with a formal dining room and crystal chandelier. I was studying Judaism intensively with the intention to convert, and I made *Seder* with Deanna, my wonderful new downstairs neighbor. Boris and I bought sixteen place settings of stoneware, flatware, and glassware, to use exclusively for Passover. I cared intensely about doing everything right, though the Passover dietary laws seemed to me unnecessarily detailed, wasteful, and sexist. My guide was a pamphlet from the Chicago Rabbinical Council, the Orthodox regulating body, which specified everything that had to be bought fresh and labeled "Kosher for Passover." I spent more money on food than I ever had in my life, feeling guilty and wondering how poverty-stricken European Jews had managed this. Yet I was determined to carry on the legacy of my mother-in-law and not be the one to break this chain of tradition. And not give anyone a reason to say, "I told you so."

Particularly fanatical that the food be authentic, I hounded Boris for menu suggestions to add to what I remembered eating at his parents' *Seder* table. I even made *gribenes,* the little cracklings left over from rendering chicken fat, horrifically unhealthy. The temple cookbook my mother-in-law had given me as a belated wedding present provided a recipe for sponge cake. I stuffed the turkey with *matzo farfel.* I made a compote of dried fruits. After all, I was a woman with something to prove: that I could make a Jewish home for my husband to rival the one he grew up in, as good as any "real" Jewish woman could make.

My father-in-law, though still in mourning, flew in for Passover and was impressed by my efforts. The table looked beautiful. Everything was kosher. I was certified as a *balabusta,* a super-housekeeper in the Jewish tradition, and 1983 became the standard for our family *Sedarim.* Since that *Seder,* each year has added memories: My fourth baby snatching the shank bone off the *Seder* plate and chewing on it. My Irish Catholic parents joining us for *Seder.* The cascade of turkey grease when we sliced through the foil roasting pan. Still, through all these years, I've never stopped resenting the dietary laws and the cleaning regimen, codified hundreds of years ago by scholarly men married to professional female servants. And I've never borne the burden of the Passover traditions with the grace I observed in my mother-in-law. But I have made it mine. ●

Passover 1999

by Angela Allyn

The visits to family.
The comfort of repetition.
The fullness of ritual,
The pleasant feeling of round when the cycle passes
   through again.
And so we sit at the table
Too long,
Everyone's vision of a perfect *Seder* eluding us.
Every year someone knocks over something
And we all yell as though the dish were broken
And cannot be repaired.
And I look around this table
And see time passing.
There are moments when you look at someone you
   know so well
When you are staring very hard into the smoke
When the fog clears and you see too much.
The future.

I see flashes of the people we are becoming,
The children gone adult
The adults grown old
And I lose the babies that my children are
Were.
I go to my scrapbooks to remember the past.
And I trace my finger over the line of our
　　collective histories.
Was it as good as it looks,
All of us smiling in our pictures?
I must remember to take pictures when we are crying
Pictures of us struggling,
Pictures of us arguing,
Part of our order
Part of the cycle
Around the table
Each year. ●

Irv and Joan Spigelman with their family, Thanksgiving 1995

Glossary

• •

All words and terms are Hebrew unless noted otherwise

afikomen *(Greek)* traditionally, a piece of *matzo* which is broken at the beginning of a Passover *Seder* and becomes the final food or "dessert" eaten at a *Seder* meal

Ahashuarus, Ahashverosh King of Persia in the *Purim* story

aliyah literally: *an ascending;* typically meaning the act of moving to Israel; also the honor of being called up to read the *Torah* in a synagogue; **aliyot** (pl.)

Ark *(English)* receptacle for the *Torah* scroll

balabusta *(Yiddish)* efficient head of household

Bar Mitzvah literally: *son of the commandment;* usually understood as a ceremony in which a thirteen-year-old boy becomes a full participant in the adult Jewish community; **B'nai Mitzvah** (pl.); the analogous female ceremony is the **Bat Mitzvah, B'not Mitzvah** (pl.)

beit din a tribunal of rabbis convened as a Jewish court of law to decide cases brought before it, as, for example, to approve a conversion

bimah raised platform or stage from which services are led

Birkat ha-Mazon the blessing recited after the meal

blintzes *(Yiddish)* (pl.) thin crepes filled with fruit or cheese

b'rachot (pl.) blessings; **b'racha** (s.)

borscht *(Russian)* soup made from beets or from beef and cabbage

break-fast *(English)* the evening meal following the fast of *Yom Kippur*

Bubbe, Bubbie *(Yiddish)* grandmother

carpe diem *(Latin)* used as an admonition to seize the pleasures of the moment without concern for the future

caveat emptor *(Latin)* let the buyer beware

challah braided bread traditionally eaten on *Shabbat* and holidays; **challot** (pl.)

chametz, chometz leavened food ritually unfit for Passover

Molly Parker, daughter of Rebecca Rubin and F. Nathan Parker, Sukkot 1996

Chanukah, Hanukkah eight-day holiday celebrating the Maccabean victory over the Syrian, Antiochus Epiphanes and the rededication of the Temple in Jerusalem in 165 B.C.E.

Chanukiah, Hanukkiah menorah holding candles used during *Chanukah;* nine candle places are for the eight days plus a *shamash,* the candle used for lighting the others; **Chanukiot, Hanukkiot** (pl.)

Chasidic, Hasidic belonging to a sect of Orthodox Jews that developed in 18th-century Poland and Russia

charoses, charoset a fruit, wine, and nut mixture used as part of a Passover *Seder* to symbolize mortar used to make bricks in Egypt

Chumash The Five Books of Moses, or *Torah* scroll, in book form

daven pray

Dayenu literally: *that would have been enough;* the response of a passage recited during Passover

dreidel *(Yiddish)* spinning top with Hebrew letters used for games during *Chanukah;* **sevivon** *(Hebrew)*

d'var Torah an explication of a section from the *Torah;* **d'vrei Torah** (pl.)

Erev eve; the time all Jewish holidays begin

Esther the Jewish queen who rescued the Jews from disaster in the *Purim* story

etrog, esrog citron/citrus fruit used with *lulav* during *Sukkot* holiday services; **etrogim, esrogim** (pl.)

farfel *(Yiddish) matzo* pieces shaped like small noodles or pellets

Four Questions *(English)* included in the Passover *Haggadah* and recited at the beginning of the *Seder,* usually by the youngest participant. Each interrogatory begins, *"Mah nishtannah halilah hazeh mikol haleylot?",* literally: *"What is different about this night from all other nights?"*

galabiyah *(Arabic)* loose-fitting women's garment with full sleeves

gefilte fish *(Yiddish)* stewed or baked fish stuffed with a mixture of the fish flesh, bread crumbs, eggs, and seasoning; prepared as balls or oval cakes boiled in a fish stock

gemütlich *(German)* comfortable; kind

gelt *(Yiddish)* recompense, money; it's a tradition to give children *Chanukah gelt* or chocolate coins

geniza storage or burial place for damaged sacred texts and religious objects

gioret female convert to Judaism

gregger *(Yiddish)* noisemaker used during *Purim* to drown out the name of Haman during the reading of the *Megillah*

Haggadah literally: *telling*; booklet used during Passover *Seder* telling of the Exodus from Egypt; **Haggadot** (pl.)

hakafa walking around the sanctuary in a celebratory parade during special occasions like *Sukkot* or *Simchat Torah*

hamantaschen *(Yiddish)* three-cornered pastry eaten during *Purim*

Haman the villain of the *Purim* story who plotted the death of the Jews

Havdalah literally: *separation*; ceremony which concludes the Sabbath or holiday

Hillel Rabbi of the Talmudic period; also organization on college campuses offering programs and services for Jewish students

Holy of Holies *(English)* central, most sacred place within the ancient Jewish Temple in Jerusalem

kibbutz a collective farm or settlement in Israel; **kibbutzim** (pl.)

Kiddush sanctification or blessing of the Sabbath and holidays recited over wine

kippah head covering which shows piety; **kippot** (pl.); **yarmulke** *(Yiddish)*

k'neidel, knaidl *(Yiddish) matzo* ball; served in chicken soup; **k'neidlach, knaidlach** (pl.)

Kol Nidre literally: *all vows*; evening service which inaugurates *Yom Kippur*

kreplach *(Yiddish)* (pl.) dough filled with meat and boiled; typically served in chicken soup

kugel *(Yiddish)* a baked pudding of noodles or potatoes, eggs, and seasonings

kvell *(Yiddish)* beam with pride

L'chaim literally: *to life;* to good health (as when offering a toast)

latkes *(Yiddish)* (pl.) potato pancakes eaten traditionally during *Chanukah*

lulav palm, willow and myrtle branches bound together and used as part of *Sukkot* holiday services

Maccabees Jewish soldiers led by Judah (the) Maccabee during events later commemorated as *Chanukah*

mandel-, mandle-, mondel-, -broit, -brot *(Yiddish)* literally: almond bread; hard cookie-like pastry made with ground nuts; the Jewish *biscotti*

maror a bitter herb used as part of a Passover *Seder* to symbolize slavery

matzah, matzoh, matzo unleavened bread eaten during Passover

matzo brei *matzo* fried with eggs and seasonings, usually eaten during Passover

Manischewitz brand of kosher wine and other Jewish foods

mechitzah, michitza a physical separation between men and women in traditional synagogues

Megillah, Megillat parchment scroll, eg: *Megillat (Book of) Esther* which contains the story of *Purim*

menorah a candelabra with seven branches

mezuzah small container of scripture affixed to the door frames of Jewish homes; **mezuzim** (pl.)

mikvah, mikveh ritual bath for purification

minyan required prayer quorum of ten Jews

Mitzrayim Egypt

Magen David, Mogen David the six-pointed star, a symbol of Judaism; also called Shield of David, Star of David; Mogen David is also a brand name of kosher wines; **Mogen Dovid** *(Yiddish)*

Mordecai Esther's uncle and a hero of the *Purim* story

Neilah concluding service for *Yom Kippur*

oy *(Yiddish)* literally: *woe;* for example, *Oy vey iz mir!* Woe is me!

Harry Goldin and his sister Joyce, c. 1958

parsha, parshah literally: *portion;* section from the *Torah* read *Shabbat* morning; also called **sedra**

pax vobiseum *(Latin)* peace to you

payis *(Yiddish)* literally: *corners;* unshorn sideburns worn by some Orthodox Jewish men; **payot** *(Hebrew)*

Pesach holiday which celebrates the Exodus from Egypt and the beginnings of the Jewish people; **Passover** *(English)*

pierogis *(Polish)* (pl.) small pastries filled with finely chopped meat or vegetables; **pirozhki** *(Russian)*

Purim literally: *lots;* the Jewish holiday celebrating Mordecai and Esther's triumph over King Ahashverosh's evil prime minister, Haman, who had drawn lots to pick the day on which he planned to massacre the Jews of Shushan; the story is read annually from the *Megillat Esther* during the *Purim* celebration

rabbi, rav literally: *my master or teacher;* a person trained in Jewish law, ritual, and tradition and ordained for leadership of a Jewish congregation; **reb, rebbe** *(Yiddish)*

rebbetzin wife of the rabbi

Rosh Hashana, Rosh Hashanah Jewish New Year usually occurring in September; beginning of the "Days of Awe" or High Holy Days, which are followed ten days later by *Yom Kippur*

s'chach natural covering for one's *sukkah*

schlep *(Yiddish)* to drag laboriously; connotation of unpleasant tasks

Seder literally: *order*; Passover dinner where the story of the Exodus from Egypt is retold; **Sedarim** (pl.)

Sephardic, Sephardim (pl.) Jews whose ancestors lived in Spain, parts of central Europe, northern Africa and parts of the Middle East; as opposed to **Ashkenaz, Ashkenazim**, those Jews whose ancestors lived in Western Europe or the former Soviet Union

Linda Mathias Kaskel and her daughter, Beth, Shabbat 1987

Shabbat Jewish Sabbath which lasts from sunset on Friday until nightfall on Saturday; **Shabbes, Shabbos** *(Yiddish)*

Shammai a rabbi of the Talmudic period whose opinions typically differed from Rabbi Hillel's

shatnes biblical prohibition of mixing wool and linen in clothing

Shema Deut. 6:4-9; 11:12-21; the central prayer of the Jewish people declaring God's unity

Shemini Atzeret literally: *eighth day of assembly*; festival at the end of *Sukkot*

shiva literally: *seven*; a seven-day period of formal mourning observed after the funeral of a close relative

shul *(Yiddish)* synagogue

Shushan city in Persia where the *Purim* story took place

shtetl village or small town in Eastern Europe where many Jews lived before World War II

Simchat Torah literally: *Joy of Torah*; festival celebrating completion and beginning of *Torah* cycle, coming after *Sukkot*

Sukkot (pl.) literally: *booths*; fall harvest festival; also refers to the fragile, temporary huts or booths built during the holiday to recall the Israelites' wanderings in the wilderness; **Sukkah** (s.)

tallit prayer shawl with ritual fringes; **tallitot** (pl.); **tallis** *(Yiddish)*; **talleisim** (pl.)

tefillin phylacteries; small boxes containing Hebrew prayers which are strapped to the left forearm and on the forehead; directive comes from the *Shema,* "and you shall bind them for a sign upon your hand . . . and they shall be for frontlets between your eyes"

Torah The Five Books of Moses; also refers to the *Torah* scroll itself, a parchment document written by a scribe and affixed to two wooden poles, or *etz chayim*

Torah she-be'al peh oral *Torah;* the compendium of Jewish law and lore traditionally given to Moses on Mt. Sinai together with the written *Torah,* **Torah she-bichtav**

treif *(Yiddish)* nonkosher food, often nonkosher meat

trope symbol indicating the musical pattern for chanting the *Torah* or *Haftorah* (The Prophets)

tsoris, tzuris *(Yiddish)* trouble

tzedakah charity given as a religious obligation

tzimmes, tsimmes *(Yiddish)* a stew of vegetables or fruits cooked slowly over very low heat; *(slang)* a state of confusion

ulpan Hebrew course

V'anachnu korim literally: *and we bow;* part of the ancient *Aleinu* prayer recited near the conclusion of the synagogue service proclaiming the unity and sovereignty of God

Vashti wife of King Ahashverosh prior to his betrothal to Esther

"Ven acá. ¡María está aquí!" *(Spanish)* literally: *"Come over here. Maria is here!"*

Yahrzeit *(Yiddish)* anniversary date of death memorialized through prayer and the lighting of a candle

yeshiva, yeshivah school or academy where traditional Jewish texts are studied; **yeshivot** (pl.)

Yiddish language spoken by Jews of eastern Europe

Yizkor memorial prayers recited by relatives of the deceased

Yom Kippur Day of Atonement marked by fasting and penitential prayers

yom tov holiday; **yontiff** *(Yiddish)*

Zadie *(Yiddish)* grandfather

Additional Jewish Holidays:

Rosh Chodesh monthly festival celebrating the New Moon

Tu Bishvat literally: *15th day of the Hebrew month of Shevat*; holiday celebrating renewal of trees and beginning of spring in Israel

Shavuot literally: *weeks*; festival occurring seven weeks after Passover which celebrates the receiving of the *Torah* at Mt. Sinai

Yom Haatzmaut Israeli Independence Day

Yom Hashoah day memorializing the *Shoah* (Holocaust)

Tisha B'Av literally: *9th day of the Hebrew month of Av*; day of mourning and fasting recalling the destruction of the Temples in Jerusalem and other tragedies

Shirley Gould (back, center) with family and friends, Thanksgiving 1958

Order Form

●●●

To order copies of any JRC Press publications, copy this page and fill out the form below. Please make checks or money orders payable to JRC, and allow up to three weeks for delivery.

_____ *Is God Still a Cubs Fan?* (updated "2000" edition)

_____ *Pirkei Imahot: A Celebration of Our Mothers*

_____ *From Oy to Joy: Our Holidays Across the Years*

1–2 books: $14.95 per book plus $5.00 shipping & handling*
3–9 books: $13.50 per book plus $7.50 shipping & handling*
10–19 books: $12.00 per book plus $10.00 shipping & handling*
20–49 books: $10.50 per book plus $15.00 shipping & handling*
50+ books: $9.00 per book plus $20.00 shipping & handling*

$_____ *Total including shipping and handling*

Ship to:

Name: _____

Address: _____

_____

City: _____

State: _____ Zip Code: _____

Phone: _____ Email: _____

Comments: _____

_____

Mail your check and order form to:
JRC Press, c/o Jewish Reconstructionist Congregation
303 Dodge Avenue, Evanston, IL 60202-3252
847.328.7678 • fax 847.328.2298 • www.jrc-evanston.org

* Books may be different titles to qualify for quantity discount,
  but all must be sent to a single address.
  Special prices available for booksellers and Jewish organizations.

*Darlene and Ray Grossman (kneeling) with Darlene's
parents, sisters, and brothers-in-law, Father's Day 1979*